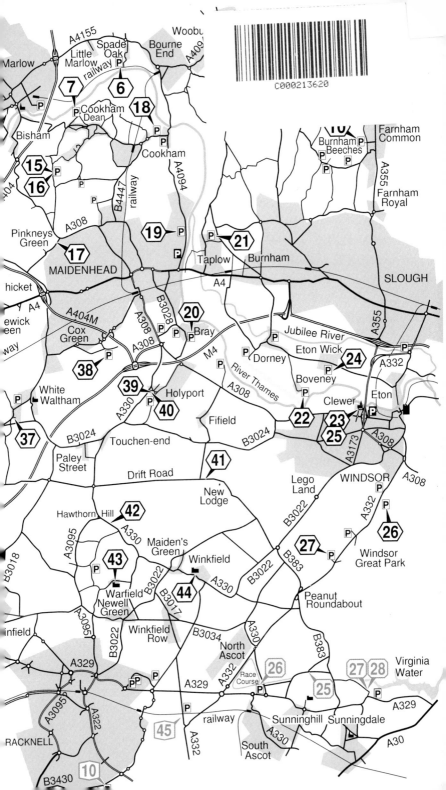

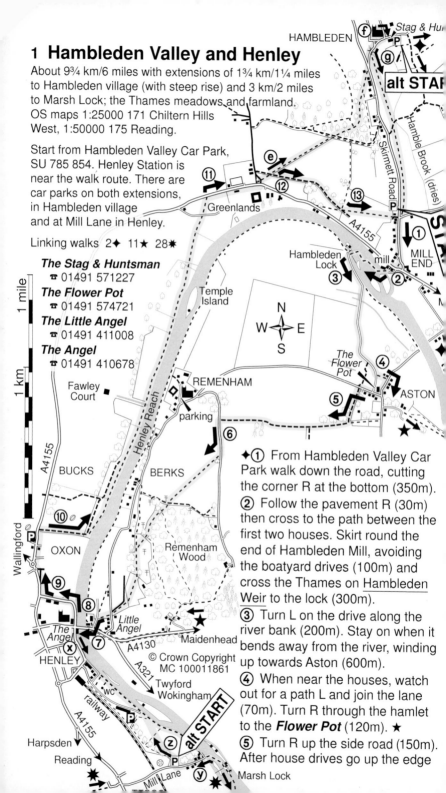

1 Hambleden Valley and Henley

About 9¾ km/6 miles with extensions of 1¾ km/1¼ miles to Hambleden village (with steep rise) and 3 km/2 miles to Marsh Lock; the Thames meadows and farmland. OS maps 1:25000 171 Chiltern Hills West, 1:50000 175 Reading.

Start from Hambleden Valley Car Park, SU 785 854. Henley Station is near the walk route. There are car parks on both extensions, in Hambleden village and at Mill Lane in Henley.

Linking walks 2✦ 11★ 28✳

The Stag & Huntsman
☎ 01491 571227
The Flower Pot
☎ 01491 574721
The Little Angel
☎ 01491 411008
The Angel
☎ 01491 410678

✦① From Hambleden Valley Car Park walk down the road, cutting the corner R at the bottom (350m).

② Follow the pavement R (30m) then cross to the path between the first two houses. Skirt round the end of Hambleden Mill, avoiding the boatyard drives (100m) and cross the Thames on Hambleden Weir to the lock (300m).

③ Turn L on the drive along the river bank (200m). Stay on when it bends away from the river, winding up towards Aston (600m).

④ When near the houses, watch out for a path L and join the lane (70m). Turn R through the hamlet to the **Flower Pot** (120m). ★

⑤ Turn R up the side road (150m). After house drives go up the edge

HAMBLEDEN

Stag & Hu

alt START

Skirmett Road

Hamble Brook (dries)

A4155

MILL END

mill

Hambleden Lock ③

②

Greenlands ⑪ ⑫ ⑬

Temple Island

N W E S

Fawley Court

REMENHAM

parking ⑥

The Flower Pot ④

ASTON ⑤

Henley Reach

BUCKS

BERKS

Remenham Wood

⑩

OXON

Wallingford

⑨

⑧

Little Angel

The Angel ⑦

HENLEY ✗

A4130

Maidenhead

© Crown Copyright MC 100011861

A321

Twyford Wokingham

wc

railway

Harpsden

Reading

A4155

Mill Lane

alt START ⓩ ⓨ

Marsh Lock

of the first field L and through the trees. On top, turn R on the track. Keep on to the next lane (950m).

⑥ Walk along the lane L watching out for the oblique side path R (200m). Follow it over the field to the edge of the wood (500m) and go on through the trees (300m). Cross the next field (80m) and drop through the trees (200m). Descend the next field towards the furthest corner (200m) and cross the next field to the lane (150m).

⑦ Cross the lane and the grass (100m) and bear L through the car park past the Leander Club to the road (100m) (or turn L along the lane). Cross Henley Bridge (150m).

ⓧ *Extension of 3 km/2 miles to* Marsh Lock: *After the **Angel** turn L and follow the road then path beside the river (1400m). ✳ Go L over the river to lock (150m).*

ⓨ *Backtrack to the bank and go up Mill Lane (350m) then R.*

ⓩ *Walk across the car park and on outside the football field (300m) then cut across the meadow R converging on the river. Keep on to Henley Bridge (1200m).*

⑧ Follow the main road along the river (150m) and round the bend up New Street to the end (200m).

⑨ Turn R along the main road (250m) and fork R on the Marlow road, A4155 (100m).

⑩ Soon after the Toll House and the Rugby Club drive (70m) take the track R to the river (400m). Turn L along the grassy river bank or the track before it. At the end cross the ditch from Oxfordshire into Buckinghamshire and carry on beside the river over more ditches and over the long narrow pond of

Fawley Court (900m) to Temple Island (700m). Keep on through the nature reserve with the river gradually curving away R (300m). At the meadow continue in the same direction, toward the cleft in the valleyside, over Greenlands drive to the main road (400m).

⑪ Go R beside the road past the college (400m). At the R bend, cross into the large track (30m) and take the oblique path R over to the hedge end in the 2nd field (70m).

ⓔ *Extension of 2 km/1¼ mile to* Hambleden *village: Ascend L of the hedge to the wood (500m). Cross the boundary tracks in the trees and keep on up the slanting path over the shoulder of the hill past a side path up L (150m). Carry on round L and down the other side to the road (400m). Turn L and fork R to the village square (200m).*

ⓕ *Go through the churchyard L of the church (100m), then R to the road and R on the road, past the side road L with the **Stag & Huntsman** and village car park, to the church square (200m). ✦*

ⓖ *Leave the square on the road you arrived by (150m) but enter the field L after the little bridge and walk down the valley from field to field, over a track (500m) to the lane with the cottage (600m). The car park is up the road (60m).*

⑫ Turn R on the level track along the R edge of the field, parallel with the road, past the clump of trees R (350m) to the very oblique cross path (250m).

⑬ Bear L on the footpath to pass 40m L of the nearest garden hedge to the road (400m). Hambleden Valley car park is L (60m).

2 Hambleden, Medmenham and the Thames

About 9¼ km/5¾ miles with a hilly extension of 2½ km/1½ miles and a short cut of 500m/¼ mile; farmland, woods and the Thames meadows.
OS maps 1:25000 171+172 Chiltern Hills West+East, 1:50000 175 Reading.

Start from Hambleden Valley car park, SU 785 854,
or the public car park behind the pub in Hambleden
or the roadside in Ferry Lane, Medmenham.

Linking walks 1✦ 3✧ 4❉ 11☆

The Stag & Huntsman
☎ 01491 571227
The Dog & Badger
☎ 01491 571362

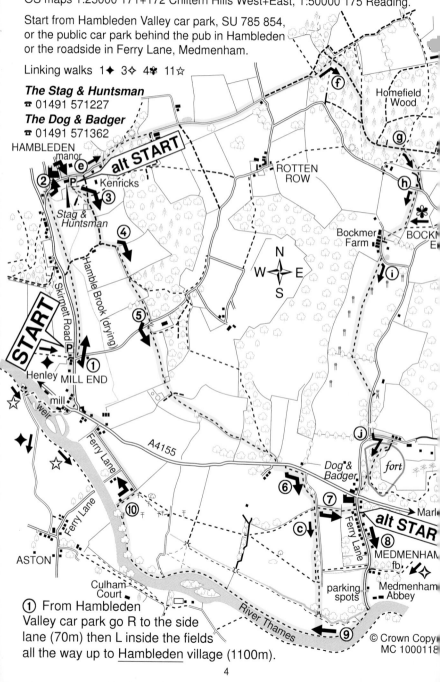

① From Hambleden
Valley car park go R to the side
lane (70m) then L inside the fields
all the way up to <u>Hambleden</u> village (1100m).

4

② Turn R. Walk round behind the church to the manor house and R to the ***Stag & Huntsman*** (200m).

ⓔ *Extension of 2½ km/1½ miles: Stay ahead, up the lane (250m), up the path in the wood (400m), along the track past sheds (200m), along the drive to the lane (650m), along the track opposite (350m). When the track bends slightly L, at the start of the wood, take the footpath inside the edge of the wood to the cross track just before the next field (200m).* ❈

ⓕ *Turn R down into the dry valley (350m). Keep on down round a broad L curve (300m) then along a straight section (200m), watching out for the small footpath crossing 200m before a large cross path.* ✧

ⓖ *Of the two paths R, bear R on the 2nd one obliquely up the valley side and pass beside a field to a converging track (200m). Stay ahead to the lane (70m).*

ⓗ *Slightly R (20m), enter the field opposite and follow the L edge (250m). At a side path L, bear R across the corner and through the next field to the farmyard (150m). Go L through the farmyard (80m).*

ⓘ *Just before the pond L enter the field R. Go straight along the middle (no visible path) to the mid-point at the far end (700m), ½L in the next field to the gate (300m) and down the lane R (300m).*

ⓙ *Turn L up School Lane (150m). At the first house turn R over a tar-mac drive and go along the track (50m). Before the field bear R into the trees (200m). At the end of the straight sloping part of the path drop off the steep edge R down to the crossroads (150m).* ➥⑧

③ Walk through the (public) car park (70m) and cross the cricket field to the far L corner (150m). Join the track outside and go R between fields to the end (300m).

④ Go L up the track into the field (100m) and R along the bottom edge to the wood (200m). Inside the wood (10m) turn R to the next field. Go L, not up the edge but up to the protruding corner of wood (150m) and carry on through the next field beside the wood (150m).

⑤ Cross the sunken lane and the drive of the pumping station to the next field (20m). After the thicket L, aim for the gap 40m R of the top corner (450m). Stay ahead over the narrow field (80m). In the next, stay level, parallel with the hedge below (250m). At the end are two fields. Continue L of the hedge, in the upper one, to the wood (300m). Go though to the next field (250m), R down the edge and over the main road (100m). Turn L (50m).

⑥ Turn into the field R. Go along the L edge (100m) and round the end to the cross path (250m).

ⓒ *Short cut of 500m, missing Medmenham: Stay ahead to the River Thames (650m).* ➥⑨ *(-400m)*

⑦ Turn L. Follow the path to Ferry Lane in Medmenham (300m).

⑧ Walk down Ferry Lane to the River Thames (700m).

⑨ Turn R. Keep to the river bank, past Culham Court (1700m) to the end of the fields (500m).

⑩ Go R along the hedge (150m), L along the lane (600m), L beside main road to the side road (200m). (path L for Hambleden Weir) ✦☆ Turn R up Skirmett Road to the car park (400m).

3 Medmenham, Bockmer and Pullingshill Wood

About 9 km/5½ miles; a splendid beech wood, farmland and a glimpse of the Thames, undulating with short steep slopes; many stiles; boggy in wet seasons at ⑪. OS maps 1:25000 172 Chilterns Hills East, 1:50000 175 Reading.

Start from Medmenham at the roadside 100m down Ferry Lane, SU 805 843, or near the river which is good for picnics. Alternatively start from one of the small car parks in Pullingshill Wood, SU 822 862.

Linking walks 2✧ 4✿ 5✲   *The Dog & Badger* ☎ 01491 571362

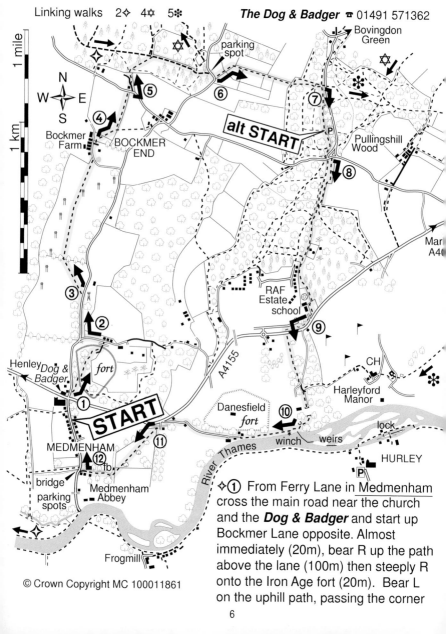

✧① From Ferry Lane in Medmenham cross the main road near the church and the *Dog & Badger* and start up Bockmer Lane opposite. Almost immediately (20m), bear R up the path above the lane (100m) then steeply R onto the Iron Age fort (20m). Bear L on the uphill path, passing the corner of a field, to the track (200m). Turn L across the tarmac drive to the houses and lane (50m).

② Go L down to the road junction (150m) then R uphill (300m).

③ Turn L up to the field at the first gate and diverge ½L from the lane to the midpoint of the cross fence (300m). Continue up the middle of the next field. Aim for the gabled cottage (700m). Go L on the drive into Bockmer Farmyard (100m).

④ Opposite the barns turn R at the 1st side track and immediately L into the field (20m). Cross the field ½R and the corner of the next field (150m). Don't go into the next field but L along the edge to the lane opposite the house (250m).

⑤ Turn R to the drive after the house (20m). Follow it (60m) then diverge R on the path in the trees (60m). Bear R in the conifer wood and go straight down into the dry valley (200m). ✿ Turn R on the forest track to the lane (450m).

⑥ Walk up the lane R (40m) and turn L into the field. Follow the fence into the valley (100m) and up to the hedge (50m). Turn R and follow the path below the hedge along the valleyside (400m). At the wood go straight up or L and round R up to the lane (200m). ✤

⑦ Just before the lane, turn R along the boundary mound down to the T-junction of lanes (500m).

⑧ Cross and take the path ahead (or the path closer to the field L) past the end of the field (350m). Carry on in the same direction, beside the boundary mound, R of a house (300m) to the school field (250m). Follow the school fence down to the A4155 (200m).

⑨ At the roadside turn R across the school drive and go on along the path in the trees into the RAF housing estate (200m). When level with the 3rd house, cross the A4155 and take the path straight over the grass, R of the clump of mature trees (200m). In the next trees (150m) cross the tarmac drive and go on down the track (40m) then on the path beside the wall, through the 50m tunnel, eventually winding steeply down to the river at one of the Hurley Weirs (300m).

⑩ Carry on beside the river past the winch (40m) to the house

> The **winch** is a replica of the one used to warp barges through Hurley flash lock. It was still usable in 1785 for the owner, Mr Pengree, was warned to have his tackle in good order while the pound lock was closed for repair. A flash lock was a gate in a weir which could be opened to let boats through. Downhill, a vessel dropped 3 or 4 feet in level. Uphill was difficult and hazardous for barges carried more than 100 tons. Weirs provided water power for mills so navigators upset production. When a barge grounded in shallows the lad could be sent upstream to ask the next miller to let out a flash of water.

(400m) then follow the drive, below Danesfield, to the road (600m).

⑪ Turn L (10m) and go down the Abbey Lodge drive (30m). After the bridge turn R into the field and cross on a line bisecting the corner. Sometimes there is no visible path. Stay more ot less equidistant from the irregular R edge and aim L of the hut (450m). Go into the wood, over a footbridge then stay beside the stream to Ferry Lane at the little bridge in Medmenham (250m).

⑫ Turn R to the main road (300m) or L to the Thames (250m). ✧

4 Pullingshill Wood and Bovingdon Green

About 9 km/5½ miles with an extension 3 km/1¾ miles via Bockmer End; tranquil farmland and splendid beech woods; steep slopes. Leaf fall obscures the woodland paths.
OS maps 1:25000 172 Chiltern Hills E, 1:50000 175 Reading.

Start near Marlow Common at one of the parking spots where the Chiltern Way crosses Pullingshill Wood SU 822 865.

Linking walks
2🌼 3✿ 5✿

The Royal Oak
☎ 01628 488611

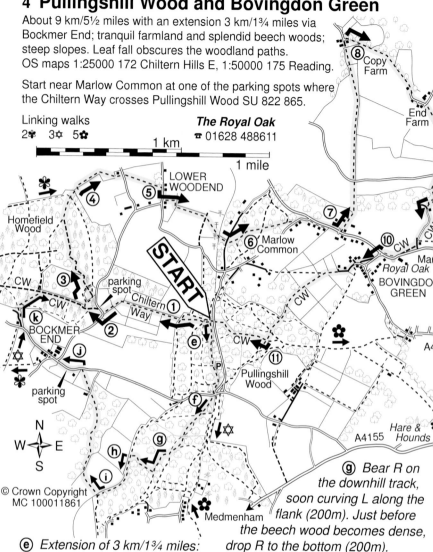

© Crown Copyright
MC 100011861

(g) *Bear R on the downhill track, soon curving L along the flank (200m). Just before the beech wood becomes dense, drop R to the bottom (200m).*

(e) *Extension of 3 km/1¾ miles: From the lane, cross the boundary mound (15m). Follow the mound L and down to the road (500m).* ✿

(f) *At the T-junction don't take the track opposite but the diverging one 20m R of it. Go into a dip and over a rise (100m) then along the brow of the hill. Watch out for a crossing boundary mound (300m). Carry on ahead to the fork (120m).*

(h) *Go L along the valley path near the fields until it bends up L at the corner of the wood (400m).*

(i) *Turn R up between fields and curve round the top of the R field (300m). Stay on the path over the top of the wood, through a dip, to the edge (400m). Cross the stable drive into the field and cross that diagonally to the corner (150m).*

8

ⓙ *Turn L on the lane to Bockmer End. Keep on past R & L side lanes (300m)* ❧ *to the first solitary house R after the hamlet (300m).*

ⓚ *Follow the drive R of the house (60m) then diverge R into the trees (60m). After the field bear R down though trees (200m). Go R on the valley track (300m) then L.* ➤⓷

① Follow the Chiltern Way over the boundary mound, away from the lane almost level (70m) then drop steeply, slightly R from a fork, to the fields (150m). Carry on ahead beside the hedge (400m).

② In the field after the hedge end go down the L edge and up to the lane in the trees (150m). Go down round the bend (50m) and L along the forest track (100m). Turn R.

③ At the nature reserve turn into the little meadow (50m) and exit at the top L gate (80m) (or take the path round outside). Follow the track up almost to the top of the valleyside where it joins a level track (600m). Turn R and soon descend into a little valley (200m).

④ Go over the valley path and up to the field (70m). Cross the corner into the adjacent field L (10m) and follow the hedge R (200m). When it bends R, cut across the corner to R of the house (100m) and follow the garden hedge to the lane (50m). In the field opposite cross slightly R. Aim for the house R of the clump of trees (300m).

⑤ Go R on the lane (100m). Just before the side lane R, turn L on the footpath between houses. Turn R & L at the end of the garden and go straight down the edge of the field into the dry valley (350m). On the other side of the track aim ½R

for the top R corner of the field (150m). Go into the wood to the vehicle track (60m).

⑥ Bear L on the path opposite and stay ahead, past side paths, to the lane at Dower Cottage (450m). Go L to the road (60m) and R down the verge (300m).

⑦ Just after Bovingdon Grange, take the path L between gardens and drop to the lane in the dry valley (350m). Go up the field opposite beside the R hedge (600m). Towards the top diverge across to the L hedge and exit at the top L corner (150m). Go on between the houses (200m).

⑧ Turn back R down the stony path beside the branch drive. Keep on to the next lane (600m) and up past houses at End Farm (100m). At the L bend, stay ahead down between fields (500m). Cross the lane in the dry valley and ascend between fields to the wood (200m).

⑨ At the path junction turn R up round to the house (80m) and L along the tarmac drive (250m). Just before the road, turn R on the track to reach <u>Bovingdon</u> Green opposite the ***Royal Oak*** (150m). Keep on along the R verge (150m).

⑩ Cross the road and the village green to the far R corner (200m). ✿ After the tarmac follow the track curving L then R to the end house (150m). Continue on the path between fields to Pullingshill Wood (400m). Stay ahead on the CW over the sunken cross path (200m) to the second cross path (80m).

⑪ Turn R (200m). After the boundary mound bear R beside it (120m) then L to the lane with the parking spots (80m).

5 Marlow, Harleyford and Pullingshill Wood

About 10¼ km/6½ miles: Thames Path, farmland, beech woods and Marlow town centre with a short cut of 1¼ km/¾ mile. OS maps 1:25000 172 Chiltern Hills East, 1:50000 175 Reading.

Start from Lower Pound Lane between the sports fields in Marlow, SU 847 861, or from one of the little car parks in Pullingshill Wood, SU 822 861.

Hand & Flowers ☎ 01628 482277   Linking walks 3✻ 4✿ 7★ 14✦ 15✻
Hare & Hounds ☎ 01628 481188
The Ship ☎ 01628 484360

① From Lower Pound Lane turn into the cricket field and R along the edge of the pitch to the river (250m). Follow the Thames Path away from Marlow, past Bisham Church (550m), Bisham Abbey (400m) and Temple Mill Island with houses (700m) to the drive (300m). ✦ (Lock & Tea Room (summer) 200m ahead.)

② Turn away from the river on the winding drive (450m). Skirt round the farm on the footpath. Keep on to East Lodge (300m).

③ Take the path L along the R edge of the field and out at the end (700m).

④ Bear R up beside the wall (Harleyford Manor visible far L) and cross the drive into the estate yard (80m). At the far wall go R up the steps (80m). Cross the drive and go on beside the golf clubhouse (bar open to the public) and round the R bend near the house (80m). Stay ahead along the Home Farm track, round a L bend to the house (100m) and on beside the golf course (300m) then down through the trees into a dip and up to a track (150m). ✻

⑤ Go up the track R to the tarmac drive (40m). Cross and stay ahead on the footpath past clumps of trees to the road (350m).

⑥ Cross into the trees at the RAF Medmenham housing estate and turn R. Keep near the main road and cross the school drive (200m).

⑦ Turn L into the trees. Follow the school fence (200m). ✿ Stay ahead on the path, past a house R (250m) to the field R (300m) and on beside it to the next road (350m).

⑧ Go up between the side roads until they join (100m) and bear R on the path into the wood near the field (200m). After the 1st field, fork R past the next field and down to a T-junction in a little valley (300m).

⑨ Go R down the valley path, out of the wood (250m), then between fields to a fork (250m).

⑩ Fork R, still in the valley, between fields down past the barn (300m) to the lane (500m). Turn L to the main road (100m).   Either

Ⓢ *Short cut of 1¼ km/¾ mile. Follow Pound Lane, opposite to Lower Pound Lane (900m). or*

⑪ Walk through Marlow: Go L on the pavement of the main road, past the **Hand & Flowers** (700m), the William Borlase Grammar School L, Shelley Cottages L (250m) and Remnantz R to the town car park (100m). Either

Ⓒ Turn L on Portlands Alley to the next road (250m) and ½R over the park and cricket field to Lower Pound Lane (200m) or **⑫** Continue beside the main road (200m) and turn R along High Street past the **George & Dragon** and church (550m). ★❋

⑬ At the side road R after the park take the path down beside the main road to the suspension bridge (80m) then follow the path along the river bank until you see the cricket field (200m). Cut across the grass aiming L of the cricket pavilion to reach Lower Pound Lane (250m).

Marlow suspension bridge opened in 1832 when local government and iron bridges were in their infancy. Parishes had been responsible for highways and bridges since 1555; manors previously. Large public bridges were usually paid for by tolls and often had income from endowments of property. Marlow was prosecuted In 1827 for not keeping the bridge in good order. The town solved the financial problem through an Act of Parliament transferring responsibility to the counties for payment by the rates (Bucks 80%: Berks 20%) and selling its bridge endowments. The estimate was £8,803. The cost was £22,000 but the sale of the endowments raised £3,000.

At that time suspension bridges were suspect because some had collapsed. William Tierney Clark, the architect, got the job because he had already built Hammersmith Bridge, and he went on to build a Danube bridge linking Buda with Pest. His apprenticeship had been at Coalbrookdale, the headquarters of Telford and birthplace of modern iron-making. The wrought iron was tested at 9 tons per square inch. Steel links were substituted in the 1960s. The previous (timber) bridges had been aligned with St Peter's Street which was the ancient town thoroughfare up from the river.

The Building of Marlow's Suspension Bridge 1828-32 D Childs 1975 98pp Shenstone College

6 Spade Oak, Little Marlow and Bloom Wood

About 7½ km/4½ miles with an extension of 3¾ km/2½ miles and short cut of ½ km/⅓ mile; long ascents but not steep; long views, wheat fields, wood and the Thames. Enid Blyton's garden can be visited at Old Thatch in Spade Oak. OS maps 1:25000 172 Chiltern Hills East, 1:50000 175 Reading.

Start from the free car park in Spade Oak, SU 883 875, or park on the verge beside the lane into Fern hamlet, SU 880 883.

The Queen's Head ☎ 01628 482927
The King's Head ☎ 01628 484407
The Spade Oak ☎ 01628 520090
The Crooked Billet ☎ 01628 521216
Old Thatch Gardens ☎ 01628 527518

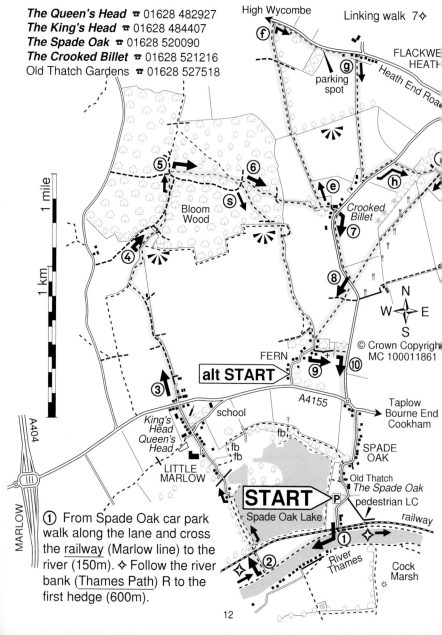

① From Spade Oak car park walk along the lane and cross the <u>railway</u> (Marlow line) to the river (150m). ✧ Follow the river bank (<u>Thames Path</u>) R to the first hedge (600m).

© Crown Copyright MC 100011861

12

② Turn R outside the hedge and re-cross the railway (200m). Stay ahead, not on the main path, but at the edge of the lake (gravel pit) 20m R. When the lake path bends R (400m) continue on the main path past houses L & R and along the lane past Little <u>Marlow</u> church (350m), the side lane with the **Queen's Head** L (150m) and the **King's Head** near the end (200m).

③ Cross the A4155. Stay ahead through the farm and beside the hedge up to the barn (750m) then over to the L hedge (150m) and up R beside it (250m).

④ Before the wood, cross into the adjacent field L but carry on in the same direction into the wood (150m). Disregard tracks L & R but join the track converging L from below (200m). A bit further on (150m) take the path diverging L up to a track junction (100m).

⑤ Bear L up the track ahead but almost immediately (15m) take the small side path R. Watch out for a path converging from the L (500m). Almost immediately after it (10m) the paths diverge again.

Ⓢ *Short cut of ½ km/¹⁄₃ mile: Take the R path over the track (40m) and carry on down through the wood (350m). At the field turn L along the top edge then cut the corner and follow the hedge down to the houses (750m).* ➧⑨

⑥ Take the L path (40m), over the track and down through the wood to the field (400m). Continue down the hedge into the little dry valley and up towards the hedge end (200m). Just before the end go through the hedge and on between fences to the side path L (50m).

The **Crooked Billet** is 80m ahead. From there, either return to the side path ➧Ⓔ or go up the road (250m) for a shortened extension ➧Ⓗ or go down the road ➧⑦.

Ⓔ *Extension of 3¾ km/2½ miles to the top of the hillside: Follow the side path up the edge of the field. Stay ahead at the L edge to the trees (450m) then at the R edge to the road (750m).*

Ⓕ *Follow the verge R (700m).*

Ⓖ *Just before the side road L at Flackwell Heath take the footpath R between gardens and carry on at the R edge of the fields all the way down to the next road (900m).*

Ⓗ *Turn L up the path on the bank of the road (250m). At the L curve cross to the path opposite. Go up the steps and the edge of the field to the top corner (200m). Carry on ahead beside the wood (100m) then R on the drive (50m).*

Ⓘ *Turn R on the track beside the fields (250m). Continue along the edge of the field (400m) and stay ahead down the slope obliquely to the road (350m). Cross.* ➧⑧

⑦ Cross to the verge opposite and follow it R downhill, soon behind trees. Continue down to the oblique cross path (500m). Turn ½R.

⑧ Follow the oblique path over the field to the houses of Fern (500m).

⑨ Just along the lane (80m) turn L on the track through the cemetery. Stay ahead to the road (250m).

⑩ Walk down the road R (350m), L on the A4155 pavement (80m) and R down Coldmoorholme Lane to Spade Oak (350m) (Enid Blyton lived at Old Thatch). Go round R&L bends to the **Spade Oak** (300m) and on to the car park (200m).

7 Winter Hill, Marlow and Bourne End

About 10¼ km/6¼ miles with an extension of ¾ km/½ mile into Spade Oak; the Thames path and riverside meadows; two steep treacherous paths; flooding in wet season. OS maps 1:25000 172 Chiltern Hills East, 1:50000 175 Reading.

Start at Winter Hill car park, SU 869 860, or Gossmore Lane car park in Marlow, SU 859 861, or Spade Oak car park, SU 883 875, or beside Quarry Wood Road in Bisham, SU 852 859.

The Spade Oak 01628 520090
The Bounty ☎ 01628 520056
The Two Brewers 01628 484140

Linking walks 5★ 6◈
  8❖ 15☆ 16❀ 18✳

© Crown Copyright
MC 100011861

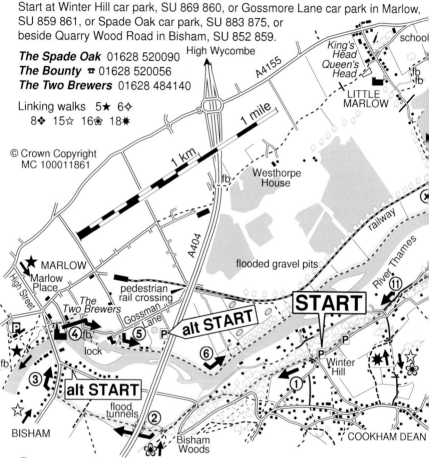

① At the top end of the Winter Hill parking area, 15m from the road, take the level path under trees (30m). At the drive turn R and skirt round the garden, above the slope in the wood (300m). Fork R at the fence corner and continue to the road (250m) but don't cross. Bear R down the steep path and cross the road at the bottom (300m). Continue on the path at the foot of the slope beside a stream (300m).

② Cross the footbridge R and the R end of the meadow to the flood tunnels (200m). Pass under the A404 and aim for the far L corner of the next field (300m). Before the corner, cut across the corner of the adjacent field (50m). Continue over the farm track and ahead between fields to the road at Bisham (200m).
③ Go R on the pavement, over a side road and Marlow suspension bridge to the church (500m). ★

14

④ Turn R into the churchyard. Go round (L of) the church to the path between walls and through to the next street (100m). Continue R of the **Two Brewers** on the zigzag

path to the next road (150m). Turn R and follow the bend (100m). Go on near the river past Marlow Lock (100m) and the mill site (200m).

⑤ Just round the L bend turn R on the tarmac path across the public gardens to the river (100m). Follow the river bank to the A404 bridge (350m) (Gossmore Lane CP L). Carry on under the road (300m).

⑥ Go round the bend in the river past the boatyard opposite (700m) and on along the meadows to the hedge end opposite the next group of houses R (1300m). ✧

ⓧ *Extension of ¾ km/½ mile to* Spade Oak*: Turn L along the hedge to the gate (200m).*

ⓨ *Just over the railway take the side path R (20m). Follow the R edge of Spade Oak Lake (500m), round the end and on to the side path R on the footbridge (300m).*

ⓩ *Turn R across the field to the* **Spade Oak** *(100m) then follow the road R back to the Thames past the public car park and over the railway lines (400m). Turn L.* ➔⑧

⑦ Stay on the river bank past the level crossing L (600m).

⑧ Continue between gardens then on the path to Bourne End (650m). After the Bourne bridge keep to the riverside (100m). When the road curves L stay with the river between fences to the railway bridge (200m). ✧ Cross the river (100m). ✹

⑨ Make for Cock Marsh behind the houses. Either pass under the bridge (30m) and back R under the railway arch (30m) or follow the river bank upstream to the **Bounty** (200m) and find the narrow path L between gardens after it (50m). Cross the meadow to the steep path up the valley side (600m).

ⓐ *Avoiding the steep path and the best views: Turn R on the track ar the foot of the slope past a side path R (400m). Stay on the track curving L up the valleyside to the little path converging L (500m).* ➔⑪

⑩ Climb the steep path from the boardwalk to the cross path below the top (100m) and turn R. Stay on this path, below the brow, mostly level, to the rising track converging from below (750m).

⑪ Continue up the track (300m). Near a side path L, where the track bends up to the house, join the footpath at the R fence. Continue between hedges (200m). ☆✿ Cross the two lanes and go up the path under trees (80m). Continue up the road (100m) then diverge R and follow the path near the road to the top car park on Winter Hill (400m).

8 Wooburn, Hedsor and Bourne End

About 7¼ km/4½ miles. Farmland slopes overlooking the Thames valley; long ascents and views. An extension of 2 km/1¼ miles follows the Berkshire bank of the Thames. OS maps 1:25000 172 Chiltern Hills East, 1:50000 175 Reading.

Start from the Park car park behind Wooburn Church, SU 910 877. Near the extension there is parking in Cookham, SU 892 853.

Linking walks
7❖ 9✦ 18✿ 19✪

The Old Bell
☎ 01628 523117
The Chequers
☎ 01628 529575
The Ferry
☎ 01628 525123
The Firefly
☎ 01628 521197

© Crown Copyright MC 100011861

① From the car park take the uphill lane outside Wooburn Park. Go round the R bend up to the L bend (300m). Just round this bend take the path R of the lane beside the garden fence up to the field (100m). Go up the field obliquely to the middle of the wood (250m). Keep on through the trees (150m) and over the top field to the corner L of the **Chequers** (100m).

Before or after the main route it is worth walking around Wooburn Church on the triangle of roads and past the **Old Bell** (400m).

16

② Go L on the road (70m) and R on the side lane (150m). When the lane bends R take the smaller side lane L (200m). This is Hedsor.

③ Turn R on the path under trees and go straight on, over the brow (100m) and down Church Path in the wood (possibly Roman road) (700m) then down the tarmac drive (100m). Lord Boston's Folly is on the hilltop R. Hedsor Church is on the hilltop L; the path to it (100m) provides excellent cardiovascular exercise and views. Carry on to the road (150m) and down the drive opposite (100m). Turn R along the cross drive before the house (100m) then L on the path through the trees and over the stream into the field (80m).

ⓔ *Extension of 2 km/1¼ mile: Bear L. The right-of-way cuts the corner to the trees (site of Hedsor Wharf) but the path is sometimes around the crop. Go on obliquely to the far L corner of the field (500m) then L along the pavement, past the toll house R. Cross Cookham Bridge into Berkshire (250m).* ✳❂

ⓕ *Just after the bridge and before the Ferry watch out for an opening R and descend to the river bank. Follow it all the way to the railway bridge (1800m).* ❖

ⓖ *Cross to the Buckinghamshire bank (150m). Turn under the bridge then back L up the steps. Keep on beside the railway to the main road in Bourne End (350m).*

ⓗ *Go L past the Firefly to the roundabout (150m) and R on Cores End Road (250m).*

ⓘ *Just before the major side road R take the path L under trees to the multiple path junction (350m).* ✦⑦

④ Bear R to follow the hedge. The right of way is straight across but sometimes the path is round the R edge of the crop. Keep on to the road (600m). Don't join it; turn R.

⑤ Follow the path diverging from the road between hedges (250m). Cross the next road and go along the farm drive opposite (250m). Carry on through the field (150m). When the path splits in the next field stay at the L edge to the end (250m) and continue ahead beside the road (100m).

⑥ Just before the bridge and the A4094, bear R on the hard path over the smaller bridge (60m) then turn R on the pavement to the side road R, Millside (150m). Cross the main road and take the path, opposite, between walls. Stay ahead up to the cross path after the housing estate (200m).

⑦ This straight level path follows the line of the old High Wycombe railway. Take the steep uphill path, avoiding the L branch, obliquely through the scrub (150m). At the field continue in the same line soon beside the L hedge (400m). At the next field change sides and keep on to the top corner next to the wood (500m).

⑧ Turn R into the adjacent field and follow the L edge (500m). In the valleyside field descend to the bottom R corner near the industrial estate (250m) and go out to the road (100m). ✦

⑨ Go L on the pavement (200m) then cross the road and the River Wey to Wooburn Park (30m). Aim for the car park L of the church (350m) or go round the edge.

9 Wooburn Green and Dipple Wood

About 6¾ km/4¼ miles with an extension of 4½ km/2¾ miles to the heath of Littleworth Common; undulating farmland and woods, bluebells in season. OS maps 1:25000 172 Chiltern Hills East, 1:50000 175 Reading.

Start from Wooburn Park car park behind Wooburn Church, SU 910 877, or, on the extension, from Littleworth Common car park, SU 936 863.

The Queen & Albert ☎ 01628 520610   **The Royal Standard** ☎ 01628 521121
The Red Lion ☎ 01628 851338   **The Blackwood Arms** ☎ 01753 645672
The Jolly Woodman ☎ 01753 644350

Linking walks 8✦ 10◇

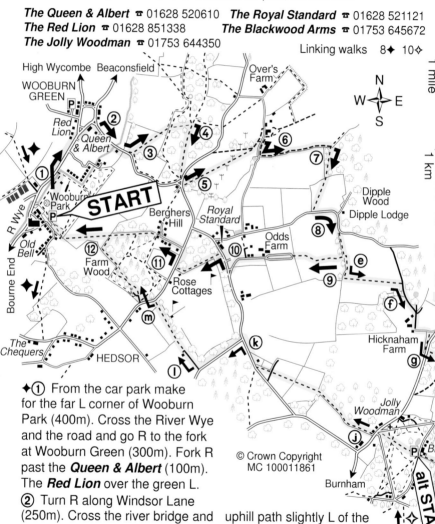

© Crown Copyright MC 100011861

✦① From the car park make for the far L corner of Wooburn Park (400m). Cross the River Wye and the road and go R to the fork at Wooburn Green (300m). Fork R past the **Queen & Albert** (100m). The **Red Lion** over the green L.

② Turn R along Windsor Lane (250m). Cross the river bridge and walk up to the R bend (100m).

③ Climb the L bank into the field and cross the slope to the hedge a little below the wood (250m). After the hedge (80m) find the gate into the wood and follow the small uphill path slightly L of the steepest line to its junction with a path rising from L and the wide path along the wood (150m).

④ From this path junction go R on the wide path, eventually rising to the road junction (400m).

18

⑤ Cross the main road to a path in the trees opposite the 2nd outlet of the side road (50m). Go through the trees and over the field to the far end of a line of trees L (600m). Go on along the farm track (50m) then cross R to the road (20m).

⑥ Join the track up the bank on the other side. Follow it R (100m), round a L bend and away from the road to Dipple Wood R (500m).

⑦ Soon after the corner of the wood (60m) turn R on the path through the wood (200m). In the next field carry on ahead to the far R corner (250m). Join the road.

⑧ Go L on the road, round the R bend at the lodge to the L bend (300m) then ahead in the field at the R edge to a side path R (200m).

ⓔ *Extension of 4½ km/2¾ mile to Littleworth Common: Stay ahead (200m) then turn L with the path over the field to the trees (450m).*

ⓕ *Follow the winding track R to the farm (250m) and turn L on the drive towards the road (100m).*

ⓖ *Outside the gateway turn R down the path beside the hedge. Carry on until the hedge meets the road (150m) then cross and find the path into the trees. Go straight across the wood to the next road (400m).*

ⓗ *Go up the road R to the T-junction (250m) and take the path into Dorney Wood opposite. The path diverges from the edge of the wood down into a dip and passes a pit (500m) to a T-junction (200m).* ✧

ⓘ *Turn R down to the field (100m). Cross up to the R corner of the*

next wood (200m) and follow the L edge of the field to the lane beside the **Blackwood Arms** (250m). Go straight on over Littleworth Common (200m). (The bridleway crossing leads R to the **Jolly Woodman** (150m) and the next path R to Dropmore Church.) Keep on to the road junction (100m).

ⓙ *Cross the main road slightly L and follow the path at the edge of the field. Stay ahead between fields then between trees and a garden to the next road (1000m).*

ⓚ *Go R along the verge (200m) then L on Sheepcote Lane (350m).*

ⓛ *At the end of the trees R, turn R along the drive. After the house continue on the path between fields to the next road (550m).*

ⓜ *Go L on the road (100m) and R on the track into Farm Wood (50m). Fork down R and cut a corner on the stepped path R of the pond (200m). Stay ahead down the edge of the wood (200m). Go round the corner R and up to the wide path (100m). Turn L.* →⑫

⑨ Take the side path R (400m). At the mobile homes stay ahead (either drive) and continue past Odds Farm to the road (500m).

⑩ Walk along the road R (150m). Just before the **Royal Standard** turn L along the path inside the edge of the wood, bending R to the next road (400m).

⑪ Go R on the road (150m) and L on the lane to houses (Berghers Hill) (200m). At the R bend stay ahead round the house and down the R edge of the wood (300m).

⑫ Cross the field to the bottom L corner (300m) and go down the next field to the car park (100m).

veney ood

od

Burnham Beeches

Dorney Wood

10 Burnham Beeches and Littleworth Common

About 7¾ km/4¾ miles, undulating through woods, farmland and heath.
OS maps 1:25000 172 Chiltern Hills East, 1:50000 175 Reading.

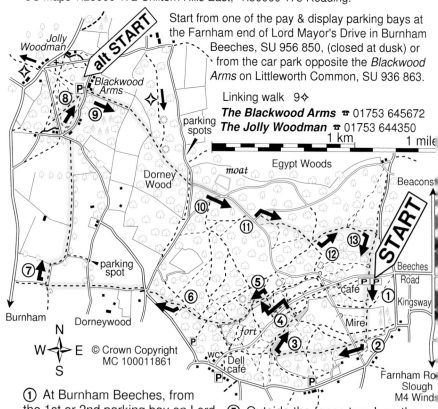

Start from one of the pay & display parking bays at the Farnham end of Lord Mayor's Drive in Burnham Beeches, SU 956 850, (closed at dusk) or from the car park opposite the *Blackwood Arms* on Littleworth Common, SU 936 863.

Linking walk 9✧

The Blackwood Arms ☎ 01753 645672
The Jolly Woodman ☎ 01753 644350

© Crown Copyright MC 100011861

① At Burnham Beeches, from the 1st or 2nd parking bay on Lord Mayor's Drive, walk straight over the grass and follow the wide path into the trees to the livestock fence (200m). Go through the gateway, along the Mire boardwalk and up to the second cross path (250m).

② Go R (80m), over the tarmac drive and straight on, eventually descending to Middle Pond (550m).

③ Cross the dam and take the path R up to Upper Pond (300m).

④ Go L up the path from the dam (80m). Over the road (20m) turn L on the parallel path (120m). Just before it ends, take the major path R across heath to the gate (100m).

⑤ Outside the fence turn L on the track along the edge of the drop (old gravel pits) (350m). When the fence finally bends L, stay ahead down into the valley (100m). Cross the valley path (Victoria Drive) and go up the other side to the path fork next to a path back R (250m).

⑥ Fork L and curve R, passing a side path L (50m). Keep on across a clearing to the road at staggered crossroads on a bend (300m). Opposite, R of the house drive, take the path along the edge of the field into a dip and up to the next road (300m). The distant large house L is Dorneywood. Cross to the field opposite and go straight over to the hedge-end (300m).

⑦ Just after the hedge corner turn R through to the other side of the hedge. Continue to the next field (150m), round the R edge and on to the end of the hedge (700m). Stay ahead up the field towards a house (200m). At the road go L up to the 4-way junction at the corner of Littleworth Common (70m).

⑧ Either follow Common Lane R (400m) or stay ahead on Dorney-wood Road to the first cross path (100m) and cross the Common R (300m) to the **Blackwood Arms**. ✧

⑨ Enter the field R of the pub and go along the edge beside the wood (300m). Cross the next field diagonally R (250m) and go up through the wood to the road (450m).

⑩ Cross into Burnham Beeches opposite and keep on along the tarmac path to the drive junction (250m). Continue ahead past McAuliffe's Drive L (300m).

⑪ At Duke's Drive turn L (60m) and take the side path R which soon broadens as it descends into the valley (450m).

⑫ Just before the bottom there is a junction of wide paths, one R and two L. Take the 2nd L (Myer's Drive) up the flank of the valley and along on the level until it curves R near the road (500m).

⑬ Just before the road, turn R on the cross path down into the valley (120m). Cross the stream (the Nile!) and go up the other side, out of the trees and over the grass to the car parks (150m).

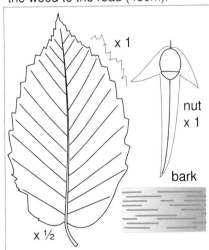

x 1

nut
x 1

bark

Hornbeam trees, *Carpinus betulus*, are scattered among the beeches in Chiltern woods. Their leaves are like beech leaves with teeth. The close-packed horizontal lenticels of 10 cm or more look like scars on the bark, a feature shared only by wild cherry in British woods. It is in the same family as hazel and has small nuts. The trifid wings are equivalent to the leafy cupules of the hazel nut. The nuts hang in jagged bunches like sycamore "keys". The split-resistant timber is used for special purposes: eg piano parts, wooden screws and snooker cues. Hornbeam is good for deciduous hedges and log fires.

Burnham Beeches is a country park of 220 ha/540 acres, bought by the City of London in 1880 but previously common land of Burnham manor. It has oak and beech woods. The striking trees are the ancient pollards. Pollarding was a way of harvesting wood from mature trees. The crown was cut off above the height of browsing animals and branches were taken on a regular cycle according to the size needed for furniture making, charcoal burning, fences, hurdles &c. The heath with birch and pine is on the Winter Hill Gravels which were the bed of the Thames at the Anglian Glaciation. Heath forms on dry soils deficient in calcium which heathers bracken and gorse can tolerate.

11 Remenham, Hambleden Weir and Aston

About 9 km/5½ miles along the Thames and over undulating farm country with long views and a bluebell wood; a short cut of 2½ km/1½ miles and an extension of 1½ km/1 mile. OS maps 1:25000 171, 1:50000 175 Reading.

Start at Remenham Church, SU 770 841. Henley Station is near the route.

Linking walks 1★ 2☆ 12❀ 28★
The Flower Pot ☎ 01491 574721
The Little Angel
☎ 01491 411008

© Crown Copyright MC 100011861

① From Remenham Church walk to the end of the side road and continue on the track to the River Thames (200m). Turn R. Follow the towpath past Temple Island (450m)

and Greenlands, the large house opposite (800m) to Hambleden Weir (700m). ☆ Go a little way over the weir towards Hambleden Mill.

② From the lock continue along the drive on the river bank to the bend (250m) then through the field ahead beside the river (600m).

22

③ At Ferry Lane turn R up past the **Flower Pot** in Aston (400m). Continue on the lane ahead.

Ⓢ *Short cut of 2½ km/1½ miles: After the houses (150m), go R up the edge of the fields (200m). On top, continue along the undulating track on the brow of the Thames valley to the next road (950m).*

Ⓣ *Walk along the road L. Watch out for an oblique side path ½R (200m) and follow it over to the edge of the wood (500m). Turn R along the edge. ➔⑫*

④ At the drive (70m) turn L to the R bend (150m) and stay ahead through the fields below Culham Court (400m) and on (250m). ✽

⑤ At the next trees take the side path R up into the spinney to the drive (300m). Cross it at the bend and go on up the next section of drive (100m). Turn R on the path up the valleyside to the gap in the top hedge at the end of the trees on the brow (450m). Look back. The large white building with tower downriver is Danesfield.

⑥ In the field on top go L along the edge to the houses (600m).

⑦ Turn R behind the gardens (350m). Cross the next field ½L (or go down the unofficial path to the gate, bottom R) (100m).

⑧ Walk down Aston Lane (250m) and take the footpath up the edge of the 1st field L to a house. Keep on to the drive junction (350m).

⑨ Turn R on the footpath beside the drive which curves L & R under trees to fields (350m). Cross the middle to the road (300m).

ⓔ *Extension of 1½ km/1 mile to Henley Bridge: Cross to the wood opposite. Stay on the main path (300m), round a curve over the drive of the R house (300m) and steeply down to the A4130 (100m).*

Ⓕ *Walk down the pavement R past the **Little Angel** (400m) and up to Henley Bridge (200m). Go out to the middle of the bridge. Either ➔Ⓧ or return (50m) ➔Ⓖ.*

Ⓧ *Extra 1 km/¾ mile to see a bit of Henley with lots of eating places: Cross the bridge (100m) ★ and go R along Thames Side (150m), round the bend and up New Street to the end (200m). ★*

Ⓨ *Turn L along Bell Street to the crossroads at Market Square (200m) and L down Hart Street past the church to the river (250m). Re-cross the bridge (150m). ➔Ⓖ*

Ⓖ *At the Leander Club drive take the tarmac side path round L to the river (80m). Follow the towpath away from Henley eventually past gardens to Upper Thames Rowing Club (950m). Keep on. ➔⑬*

⑩ Walk down the lane R past the next house L near the end of the wood (350m).

⑪ At the end of the garden take the path L under trees to the field (100m) and carry on at the edge of the wood over a cross path (250m).

⑫ Carry on to the corner of the wood (100m) and ahead across to the hedge (100m). Turn R down to the lane (80m) and cut through the rowing club opposite to the river bank (50m). Turn R.

⑬ Stay on the Thames Path past Fawley Court opposite (500m) and Remenham Church R (100m).

⑭ Further on (100m), just before Remenham Manor, turn R on the path to the lane and church (200m).

12 Crazies Hill, Culham and the Thames

About 8½ km/5½ miles with an extension of 2 km/1¼ miles; along the Thames and up the valleyside. OS maps 1:25000 171 + 172, 1:50000 175 Reading.

Park near the *Horns*, Crazies Hill, on the verge of Hatchgate Lane, SU 800 809.

Linking walks   11✻   13✻   14✳

The Horns ☎ 01189 406222

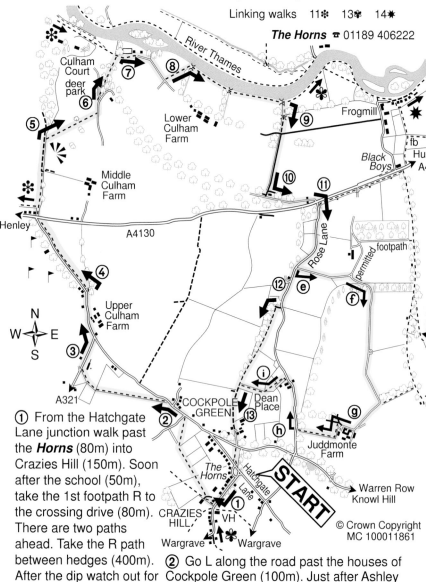

① From the Hatchgate Lane junction walk past the ***Horns*** (80m) into Crazies Hill (150m). Soon after the school (50m), take the 1st footpath R to the crossing drive (80m). There are two paths ahead. Take the R path between hedges (400m). After the dip watch out for the oblique side path R before the end field and follow it between fences to the road (200m).

② Go L along the road past the houses of Cockpole Green (100m). Just after Ashley Hill Place (30m) climb the bank to the footpath L and diverge from the road beside the fence (500m). Stay beside the hedge through the cricket field to the road (150m).

③ Turn R to the T-junction (250m) and L on the road past Upper Culham Farm (300m).

④ At the L curve, just before the field R, take the path R in the trees into the corner of the field and go on at the L edge (600m). Cross the A4130 into the field beside the end house. ✳ Follow the R edge away from the road to the track bend (350m) and ahead (120m).

⑤ Just before the track curves L at the trees, turn into the adjacent field R (Culham deer park) and descend slightly L to the estate road in the dry valley (400m).

⑥ Go L on the road (70m). At the R curve stay ahead (30m) then bear R over another drive down the path though the spinney to the path from Culham Court (300m).

⑦ Turn R past the cottages (150m) and continue on the estate road to the junction (250m).

⑧ Turn L on the path to the River Thames (200m). Cross the ditch and carry on beside the river over another ditch (300m) to the field after the third ditch (400m). ✳✳

⑨ Turn R across the end of the field (80m) and stay ahead through the belt of trees, up the R edge of the field (150m), over a hard track and up to the tarmac drive in the trees (400m).

⑩ Go L on the drive, past the lodges to the A4130 (400m).

⑪ Cross and walk up the winding Rose Lane (500m). Just past the top of the rise is the stud farm gate & drive L - a permitted footpath.

ⓔ *Extension of 2 km/1¼ mile on stud farm drives with long views: Go down the drive to the 3-way junction (400m).*

ⓕ *Bear R up round a R curve. Keep on (950m) and round a R bend to Juddmonte Farm (250m).*

ⓖ *Turn R on the tarmac side drive beside the buildings (80m). When the drive bends to the buildings, bear R on the track and fork L but, almost immediately (30m), take the footpath L along the hedge outside the end of the field (100m). Go R along the 2nd side and through trees to the road (300m).*

ⓗ *Walk down the road R (350m).*

ⓘ *Just round the bend at the houses take the path L up the field next to Dean Place to the top of the slope (150m) and R along the edge of the top field to the track (200m). Turn L. ➔⑬*

⑫ Stay ahead on the lane through the dip (100m). After the house R (200m), at the twist in the lane turn R & L up the bridleway in the trees. Continue up the flank of the dry valley to the top (650m) and ahead.

⑬ Follow the farm track to the road at Cockpole Green (400m). Go straight on across the green (150m) then along Hatchgate Lane L to the *Horns* road junction (50m).

Mortality in Nature: If two blackbirds live for 4 years producing two clutches of 5 eggs per year, they ought to be survived by 40 offspring. However, if the population is constant, on average 38 must die. If a pair of fish produce 100,000 eggs, 99,998 must die. Each fern and toadstool releases millions of spores each year; an old oak will drop millions of acorns in its lifetime; almost all die. The competition within species is far greater than between species as the individuals have the same needs. Recognition of survival of the fittest allowed Darwin to propose a plausible mechanism for evolution. The idea of evolution itself was not new.

13 Frogmill, Bowsey Hill and the Thames

About 9 km/5½ miles with a short cut of 4¼ km/2¾ miles and an extension of 2½ km/1½ mile; along the Thames and up the valleyside; farmland; woodland on Bowsey Hill. OS maps 1:25000 171+172+160, 1:50000 175 Reading.

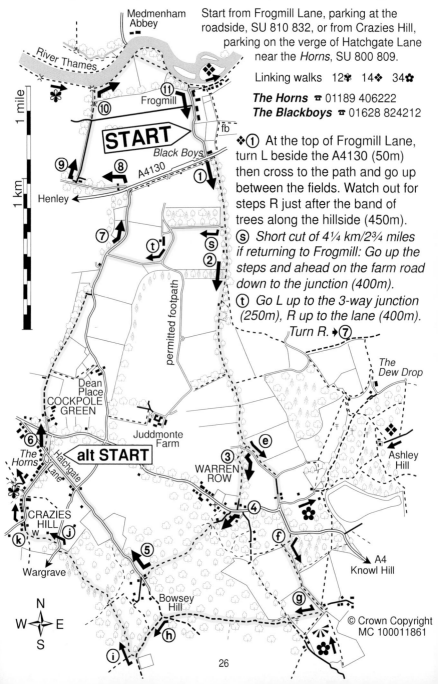

Start from Frogmill Lane, parking at the roadside, SU 810 832, or from Crazies Hill, parking on the verge of Hatchgate Lane near the *Horns*, SU 800 809.

Linking walks 12✽ 14❖ 34✿

The Horns ☎ 01189 406222
The Blackboys ☎ 01628 824212

❖① At the top of Frogmill Lane, turn L beside the A4130 (50m) then cross to the path and go up between the fields. Watch out for steps R just after the band of trees along the hillside (450m).

Ⓢ *Short cut of 4¼ km/2¾ miles if returning to Frogmill: Go up the steps and ahead on the farm road down to the junction (400m).*

ⓣ *Go L up to the 3-way junction (250m), R up to the lane (400m). Turn R.* ◆⑦

© Crown Copyright
MC 100011861

N
W E
S

26

② Stay ahead. Avoid the L fork (350m). Pass a chalkpit L (200m), a side path R in the trees (400m) and a side path L between fields (80m). Watch out for the next side path R at a slight L bend (400m).

ⓔ *Extension of 2½ km/1½ miles: Stay ahead between fields round the curve (300m), over the farm road at the L bend, past the houses (200m), ♣ up the L fork of the lane to the road (50m) and on to the L bend (200m).*

ⓕ *At the bend take the winding path R in the trees (120m) then L into the field (10m). Follow the L edge (300m) and keep on between fields to the cottage L (200m).*

ⓖ *At the bend enter the field R. Don't follow the L edge but diverge ½R to the trees at the middle of the opposite edge (250m). In the wood, slightly L (20m), carry on in the same direction on the uphill track to the 4-way track junction on top of Bowsey Hill (850m).*

ⓗ *Just after the track back L (20m) turn down the other L track (350m).*

ⓘ *On the L bend just after a little rise, take the footpath R. Avoid the branch path L (20m) and continue, undulating and winding through trees, over cross paths (400m) ahead to the next road (500m).*

ⓙ *Go R on the road round the bend (50m) then L on the path into the trees. Continue ahead, past* Rebecca's Well, *to the road at Crazies Hill village (300m).*

ⓚ *Go up the road R, round the bend to the village hall (150m) ✿ and ahead past the* **Horns** *to Hatchgate Lane (300m) & L.* ➜⑥

③ Go R on the side path, over the farm road and through trees (80m),

round a L bend and beside the field then between houses to the road at Warren Row (400m).

④ Turn R (50m) and take the next side track L between the houses (100m). After the cottage continue on the main uphill path to the lane and houses on Bowsey Hill (600m).

⑤ Walk down the lane R past the crossroads (800m) past the side road at Crazies Hill village near the **Horns** (250m).

⑥ Soon after the junction (40m) take the path R across the end of Cockpole Green (150m). Continue, over the road, on the farm drive under the trees. Stay ahead along the track to the brow of the hill (400m) and down the bridleway between fields to the road (600m). Go L on the winding road, past a cottage (200m), and up (100m).

⑦ Carry on over the rise and down to the A4130 (400m).

⑧ Cross to the drive opposite. Go L past the lodges to the first long side track R out of the wood (400m).

⑨ Turn R on the track. Stay ahead down the L edge of the field (400m), over a major track to the corner (120m), through the belt of trees and across the end of the narrow meadow to the River Thames (100m).

⑩ Follow the river bank R until opposite the end of Ferry Lane in Medmenham (400m). Either bear R across the river bend (250m) or stay on the bank round opposite Medmenham Abbey (350m). Keep on to Frogmill (300m).

⑪ Take the short path R towards the first buildings (20m). Zigzag through the byway and walk up Frogmill Lane (450m to the A4130).

14 Hurley, Ashley Hill and the Thames

About 8¼ km/5¼ miles with extensions 1¾ km/1 mile to Burchett's Green and 2¼ km/1¼ miles: farmland, river meadow and a bluebell wood: one short steep ascent. OS maps 1:25000 172 Chiltern Hills East, 1:50000 175 Reading.

Start in Hurley from the public car park opposite the church, SU 825 840, or in Burchett's Green from the parking area beside the school, SU 838 812.

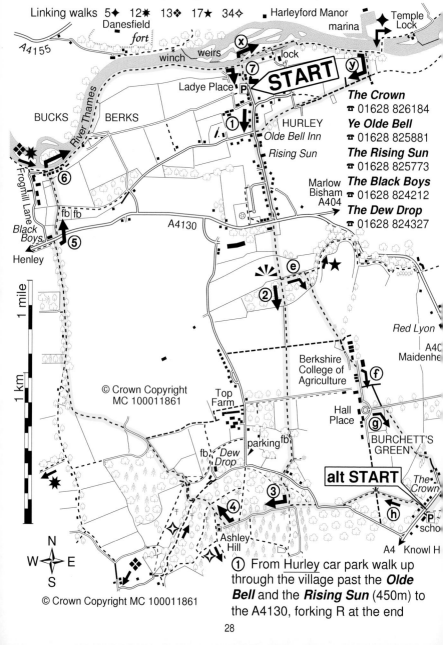

Linking walks 5✦ 12✱ 13❖ 17★ 34◇

The Crown
☎ 01628 826184

Ye Olde Bell
☎ 01628 825881

The Rising Sun
☎ 01628 825773

The Black Boys
☎ 01628 824212

The Dew Drop
☎ 01628 824327

© Crown Copyright MC 100011861

© Crown Copyright MC 100011861

① From <u>Hurley</u> car park walk up through the village past the *Olde Bell* and the *Rising Sun* (450m) to the A4130, forking R at the end

(400m). Cross and go up the path to the brow of the hill (400m). ◥◢

> The large white building with a tower on the far side of the Thames valley, is Danesfield. Far R, round the bend in the valley, the white square tower is Bisham Church, with the tall spire of Marlow Church beyond it.

ⓔ *Extension of 1¾ km/1 mile to Burchetts Green: Turn L along the path on the edge of the hill (200m) ★ then R across the wood (120m), down into the (dry) valley and up to Berkshire College of Agriculture (400m). When the hard track bends R (200m) stay ahead on the path to the farm road (30m).*

ⓕ *Follow the farm road R to the big house, Hall Place (300m).*

ⓖ *Turn L on the main drive (70m). Opposite the side track L, turn R over the field diverging from the R edge towards a house behind a clump of trees (400m). Follow the path R of the garden (100m) then the lane to the* **Crown** *in Burchett's Green (200m). Turn R up the road to the school and car park (200m).*

ⓗ *Opposite the car park take the path between gardens and stay ahead on the irregular path (400m). Cross the track L of the bridge and continue at the R edge of the field into the trees (250m). Walk up the road R (200m). When it bends R take the path ahead up to the drive (150m). Carry on ahead.* ➔③

② Stay ahead in the wood (200m), through fields, over a farm track (300m) and a farm road (350m, up the middle of the field into the trees (200m, and up the L edge of the field to the lane at houses (300m). Cross and go up the path in the wood to the drive (200m). Turn R.

③ Walk up the drive to the house on top of Ashley Hill (500m). ❖❖✳

④ Turn R on the path over the brow and down (300m). Cross the broad bridleway and carry on down the winding footpath, past a house R (100m) then down the zigzag edge of the wood (400m). Bear R on the farm road up the slope to the R bend (200m) then L on the path outside the top of the fields (500m). Curve R from the ridge down to the converging path in trees (200m). Stay ahead down (850m).

⑤ Cross the A4130 slightly R (30m) and take the path along the L edge of the fields. Skirt round gardens to the river (500m).

⑥ Turn R on the riverside track past the houses (150m). Continue on the river bank below Danesfield and the cliffs on the opposite side and past weirs to the T-junction of paths at the footbridge from the island at Hurley (1700m).   Either:

⑦ Turn R on the path past houses to Hurley church L, car park and Ladye Place R (150m).   or:

ⓧ *Extension of 2¼ km/1¼ mile along the Thames: Cross to the island and continue beside the river past Hurley Lock (200m) to the end of the island (200m). Re-cross and go on along the river bank watching out for the side path through the trees R 100m before Temple Footbridge (500m).* ✦

ⓨ *Turn R along the path away from the river (150m) and R on the track near the house. Stay ahead all the way to Hurley: track then tarmac drive (550m) then footpath between fields and gardens (300m). At the village street turn R to the car park (300m).*

15 Cookham Dean and Quarry Wood

About 6¾ km/4¼ miles; farmland and woods, undulating. The extension of 1½ km/1 mile to Bisham has a nasty road crossing. OS maps 1:25000 172 Chiltern Hills East, 1:50000 175 Reading. Linking walks 5✳ 7☆ 16✳ 18✿

Start from the layby at Cookham Dean Common, SU 861 843 (on Winter Hill Road). On the alternative section park at Winter Hill car park, SU 869 860.

Sanctum on the Green 01628 482638   ***The Chequers*** ☎ 01628 481232
Uncle Tom's Cabin 01628 483339   ***The Bull*** ☎ 01628 484734

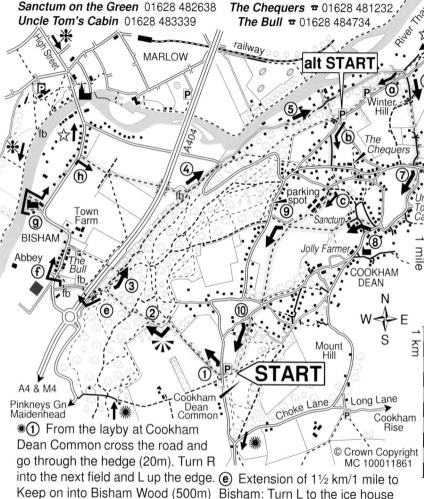

✳① From the layby at Cookham Dean Common cross the road and go through the hedge (20m). Turn R into the next field and L up the edge. Keep on into Bisham Wood (500m) to the first cross path (30m).

② Turn L (60m) and R outside the corner of the field (80m). When the main path curves L stay ahead on the minor path down to a bridleway (150m). Cross it slightly L and drop steeply to the bottom (250m).

ⓔ Extension of 1½ km/1 mile to Bisham: Turn L to the ice house and cottages (100m). Go along the lane (70m). Just round the bend, bear R up the path in the trees (20m). Cross the dual carriageway slightly R (30m) and go along the lane past the 1st footbridge to the 2nd (150m). Cross and continue

30

ahead then find a path L to the road opposite Bisham Abbey, the National Sports Centre (100m). Cross to the pavement.

(f) Walk R through the village past the **Bull** (150m) and round a L bend (150m) to the R bend (250m).

(g) Go down the side road and L of the church to the Thames (100m). Follow the bank R (70m) and return to the main road via the path outside the churchyard (150m). Go on along the pavement to the end of the field R (500m). ✿

(h) Cross into the field and follow the L edge (200m). After the farm track aim slightly L to the flood tunnels (400m). Pass under the road, slightly L across the end of the field and over the footbridge into the wood (200m). Turn L. ➔④

③ Turn R (30m) and fork down L on the track along the foot of the hill past a footbridge L (800m).

④ Go on near the stream (300m). Cross the road (nasty bend) and follow the tarmac lane, Quarry Wood, soon near the Thames then above the riverside houses (550m).

⑤ At the end of the tarmac, bear R on the path which soon joins a track above the boatyard (300m). (A path L drops to the river at the boatyard. A very steep scramble up beside the fence R leads to Winter Hill top car park.) Carry on, soon on tarmac, and eventually curve R up to the road (550m). ✿

(a) Alternative via Winter Hill 500m shorter: 30m before the road take the path R up through the trees (50m). Continue up the road (100m) then bear R. Follow the path near the road up to the top car park on Winter Hill (200m).

(b) Walk along the road past the steep lane L and houses (150m) then turn L down Job's Lane, a steep track with houses (200m). Cross the road at the bottom and go on to the next road (120m).

(c) Turn R to the bend (100m) then take the track L skirting round the farm buildings & house to the path junction in the field (450m). ➔⑨

⑥ Cross the road and go along the track past the houses (200m). When the track bends R stay ahead on the path, over a farm track, across the field (200m) and down the track between gardens to the road in Cookham Dean (200m).

⑦ Cross slightly L (20m) and go up Warners Hill. The side path R cuts across a curve (300m). Turn R past **Uncle Tom's Cabin** and take the path looping around the L edge of the green (80m). Rejoin the road and go round the S-bend (100m).

⑧ Just after Popes Lane, bear R up the track at Old Cricket Green. Don't stay on the track but cross the grass obliquely to the middle at the top and continue past (R of) the **Sanctum on the Green** (150m). Carry on under the trees (150m). and into the field R. Descend to the 4-way path junction in the dry valley (300m). Turn L.

⑨ Follow the valley path up to the road (500m) and continue on the side lane opposite (150m).

⑩ Turn L up the side lane to the cluster of houses (not the footpath beside the lane) (60m) and follow the path R beside the hedge of the top house to Cookham Dean Common (80m). Skirt round the R edge to the car park (300m).

16 Cookham Dean Common and Bisham Woods

About 8 km/5 miles; undulating woods and farmland. The extension into Cookham Dean of 3¼ km/2 miles and the short cut of 4¼ km/2½ miles can be used together. OS maps 1:25000 172 Chiltern Hills East, 1:50000 175 Reading.

Start at the Cookham Dean Common layby, SU 861 843 (on Winter Hill Road).

Sanctum on the Green ☎ 01628 482638   *The Jolly Farmer* ☎ 01628 482905
The Arbour ☎ 01628 797777   *The Golden Ball* ☎ 01628 580212

Linking walks
7❋ 15✳ 17✲

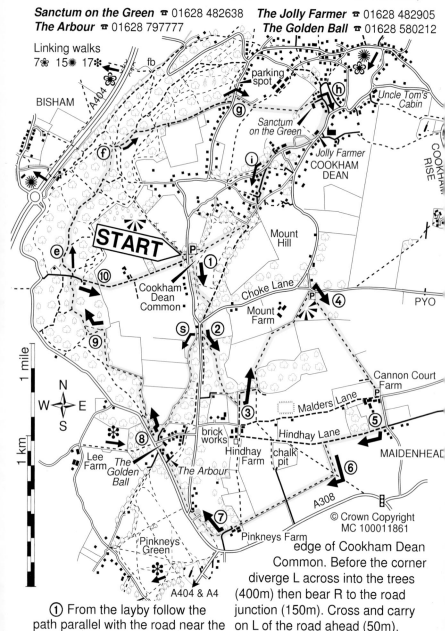

① From the layby follow the path parallel with the road near the edge of Cookham Dean Common. Before the corner diverge L across into the trees (400m) then bear R to the road junction (150m). Cross and carry on L of the road ahead (50m).

Ⓢ *Short cut of 4¼ km/2½ miles: Cross the road into the trees after the house. Follow the path at the R edge of the wood (700m) then the track from the house to the road junction (150m). Turn R.* ✦Ⓑ

② Diverge L into the trees. Stay ahead (450m) and L of a garden corner to the field (100m).

③ Turn L and skirt round the field to the cross path at the bulge of the next wood (200m). Cross to the field L (25m). Carry on at the R edge to the corner of the wood and across obliquely (300m). Bear R beside the hedge (200m) and L up the next field (Windsor Castle and Cliveden far R) to the road (250m).

④ Turn R, away from the road, down the long straight track to the end at Cannon Court Farm (900m). Continue on the lane ahead to the houses (250m).

⑤ Go R on the track past the little wood R to the field end L (450m).

⑥ Turn sharp L up the hedge to the path junction on top (250m). Turn R into the adjacent field and follow the path beside the L hedge, over the chalkpit track and through the next field to the tree-lined edge near Pinkneys Farm (750m). Stay ahead on the track (200m). ✱

⑦ Just round the L bend, turn R in the trees. Follow paths on the grass R of the main road (the edge of Pinkney's Green) over Winter Hill Road (300m) and past the **Arbour** and **Golden Ball** (500m).

⑧ From Golden Ball Lane walk along the R edge of the main road (100m). After the houses turn R on the path through the wood (150m). Just before the track from the gate L, turn R on the side path. Keep to the winding path at edge of the wood outside fields (800m).

⑨ Stay on the path when it bends L away from the fields beside a boundary mound (100m). Turn R at the main path and stay on it to the gate and vehicle track (450m).

ⓔ *Extension of 3¼ km/2 miles to* Cookham Dean: *Cross into the next part of* Bisham Woods *and follow the main bridleway.* ✳ *When it bends R at a right angle (750m) stay ahead down the steepening path to the track junction (250m).* ✿

ⓕ *Don't turn R up the steep path but bear R on the other rising path. Disregard the first R fork (50m) but bear R at the next fork (120m). Keep on up, over the brow (200m) and down beside a field (450m).*

ⓖ *Before the road watch out for a side path L and cut the corner (80m). Over the road take the path down the L end of the field (150m). Cross the valley path and go up the other side into the trees (350m) then L to the* **Sanctum** *(150m).*

ⓗ *Follow the track ahead then R round the top of the green (130m) and go R up the road (300m). After the church and* **Jolly Farmer**, *fork R. Keep on past the school (250m) to the track with houses L (150m).*

ⓘ *Go along the track (300m), over the road at the bend and along the lane (150m). When it bends R take the path ahead through the trees and cross the Common, L of the tree clump, to the car park (450m).*

⑩ Turn R on the track past the house to the edge of the wood (200m). Carry on between fields (650m). Before the road turn L along the hedge (50m) and R over the road to the car park (20m).

17 Burchett's Green and Pinkneys Green

About 9½ km/6 miles with an extension of 1½ km/1 mile through Maidenhead Thicket; a short cut of 1½ km/1 mile is shown on the map. Undulating farmland and woods. OS maps 1:25000 172 Chiltern Hills East, 1:50000 175 Reading.

Start at Pinkneys Green cricket field parking area, SU 862 822, or at Burchett's Green from the car park beside the school, SU 838 812.

The Crown ☎ 01628 826184
The Arbour ☎ 01628 777779
The Shire Horse ☎ 01628 825335

The Golden Ball ☎ 01628 580212
The Stag & Hounds ☎ 01628 630268

Linking walks 14★ 16✳

From the parking area cross the cricket field past the pavilion and go on beside the trees at the L edge of Pinkneys Green until the path bends slightly L (150m).

(e) *Extension of 1½ km/1 mile via Maidenhead Thicket: Fork L to the corner of the green (150m). On the the lane turn L and fork R past the* **Stag & Hounds** *(150m). Go round the corner R at the main road (50m) then cross to the green and follow the path diverging from the road through trees and over a lane to the meadow (200m). Follow the L edge past curving paths from the houses L to the long straight path L, ¾ of the way along (600m).*

(f) *Look across the meadow R for the exit through the trees and bear R on the path to it (200m). Go over the road and ahead (100m), then R & L over the A404 footbridge to the horse track (150m).*

(g) *Turn R (40m) and take the next side path L (200m). Fork R to a larger cross path (50m) and turn L. Keep on, L at the fork, to the horse track beside the A4 (350m). Follow it R to the corner of the wood opposite the* **Shire Horse** *(200m).*

(h) *Turn R with the horse track (80m). Near the corner of the field diverge L on the little path in the* trees. Cross the bridleway (50m) and continue near the edge of the wood past Stubbings House to path junction at the Lodge (600m).

(i) *Turn L across both drives. Continue along the very narrow field (250m) and ahead. ➤(5)*

(1) Continue ahead, diverging from the trees (150m). Cross the road and follow the track, Bix Lane, to the next part of green. Stay ahead (200m) over the lane and along the R edge of the green, L of a house. Carry on along the grassy path R of the thicket to the field R (300m).

34

② Turn R along the path outside the field to the graveyard (250m) then make your way L of Stubbings Church to the road (200m).

③ Go L along the pavement to the end of the field (200m) then cross the road and follow the track L of the drive of Stubbings House (150m). Drop to the drive to pass under the A404.

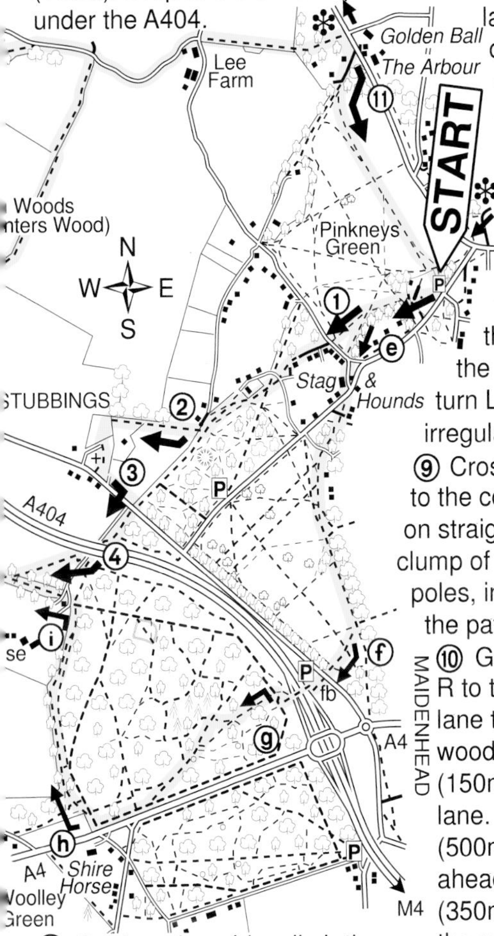

④ On the other side, climb the zigzag path R to the field (100m). Cross diagonally to the L hedge before the corner (250m). Bear R.

⑤ Continue on the farm track to the road at Stubbings Farm (750m). Turn R to the crossroads (80m).

⑥ At Burchetts Green crossoads take the lane opposite the **Crown** to the end (200m). Bear L along the garden hedge (100m) and cross the field to the BCA drive at the far L corner (400m). See Hall Place L.

⑦ Turn L on the drive (100m) then R on the side drive through the college farm (300m). At the very large shed R bear L on the diverging side path (50m) and continue along the farm road and tracks to the dip after the buildings (150m). Stay ahead up the path between fields (400m) and through the wood to the end fence (100m).

⑧ Turn R on the side path through the wood (100m) then L down round the edge of the trees (500m). After the house turn L beside the trees up round the irregular edge to the gate L (500m).

⑨ Cross the A4130 into the golf club to the corner of the club house. Carry on straight down the grass, R of the clump of trees and 40m R of electricity poles, into the trees (400m). Follow the path L to the underpass (200m).

⑩ Go under the A404 (70m) and R to the lane (70m). Just up the lane take the path R up into the wood (30m). Keep to uphill paths L (150m) & L (450m) back to the lane. Keep on (R) to the T-junction (500m). Opposite, take the path ahead at the R edge of the field (350m) then through the trees to the road (200m) near the **Golden Ball** and the **Arbour**. ✳

⑪ Turn R beside the road (50m), R on the track with houses (100m) and L across Pinkneys Green on the path parallel with the road to the cricket field (700m).

Golden Ball
The Arbour

Lee Farm

Woods
nters Wood)

N
W — E
S

Pinkneys Green

START

Stag & Hounds

STUBBINGS

A404

se

Shire Horse
Woolley Green

MAIDENHEAD

A4

fb

M4

18 Cookham, Cock Marsh and the Thames

About 7 km/4½ miles with extension of ¾ km/½ mile to the old part of Cookham Dean and a short cut of 1½ km/1 mile; long views; a hazardous steep descent. OS maps 1:25000 172 Chiltern Hills East, 1:50000 175 Reading.

Start from the car park on the Moor at Cookham, SU 892 853.

The Crown ☎ 01628 520163
The King's Arms ☎ 01628 530667
The Bounty (part time) 01628 520056

The Ferry ☎ 01628 525123
Bel & The Dragon ☎ 01628 521263

Linking walks 7✸ 8♣ 15✿ 19★

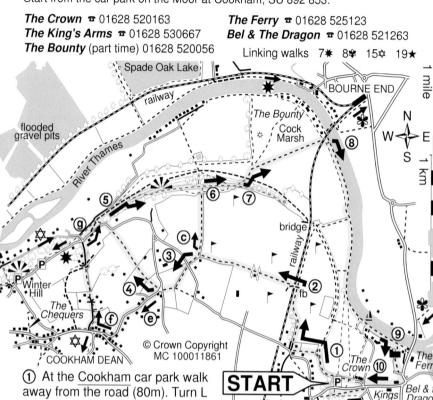

© Crown Copyright MC 100011861

① At the Cookham car park walk away from the road (80m). Turn L over the footbridge before the field and carry on round the foot of the slope (200m). Take the first side path L up between fences (200m). Don't join the lane but turn back R along the track (60m) and continue on the footpath in the field curving L to the railway fence (300m). Keep on to the footbridge L (150m).

② Cross the railway and continue ahead to pass R of the golf course shed (300m) up to a hedge corner (150m). Carry on beside the hedge to the end, near a house L (250m) and cross into the next field.

ⓒ *Short cut of 1 km/¾ mile: Turn R along the hedge into the corner (400m) and drop over the brow of the hill to the contour path just below (40m). Turn R.* ➔⑥

③ Turn L along the hedge to the road (100m). Cross into the field ahead and follow the R fence to the bend (200m) then bear R on the path between hedges to the road junction (100m).

36

ⓔ *Extension of ¾ km/½ mile: Go straight down Alleyns Lane ahead to* Cookham Dean *(500m).* ✿

ⓕ *Follow the road R (100m). At the field, turn R up the track or the footpath R of it. Keep on up past house drives to the top (200m) and over the field at the R edge (200m). At the next houses cross the track and follow the shared drive ahead to the road (200m).* ✳

ⓖ *Follow the road R up to the house & barn (70m) then diverge L down the track to the path junction (80m). Continue on the track.* ➤⑤

④ From the road opposite (10m) take the path R between fields to the next road at a bend (500m). Follow the road L to the next bend (60m) then drop R down the steep path (60m) and go R on the track.

⑤ Disregard the side path down L (200m) but after it (100m) diverge R up the side path round the trees. Carry on along the contour just below the brow of the valleyside, passing lesser paths up R and a path dropping almost straight from the field above (500m).

⑥ Continue on the contour path overlooking Bourne End across the Thames. Identify the end corner of the large field on the flat area below (200m).

⑦ Before the corner, bear L down the very steep path to the board-walk (100m). Follow the boardwalk out onto Cock Marsh then bear R towards the end of the hedge near the river (600m). Pass under the railway arch (30m) and turn L to the River Thames (30m). ✿ The ***Bounty*** is 200m L along the bank.

⑧ Follow the river bank R almost to Cookham Bridge (1600m).

⑨ Turn R at the garden wall. Pass through the churchyard and turn L to the main road (250m). Go R round bends past the Tarrystone L to the Stanley Spencer Gallery and the ***Bel & the Dragon*** R (100m). ★

⑩ Turn R along Cookham High Street past the ***Kings Arms*** and Stanley Spencer's house L to the Moor (300m). Continue ahead either along the causeway from the war memorial L or round the edge of the Moor from the ***Crown*** R until level with the car park (250m).

Swan Upping has been associated with Cookham for a century because the King's or Queen's Swan Markers have been Cookham men. Upping is the marking event, largely ceremonial in recent times. The birds are driven against the bank and captured while the cygnets are still in family groups and ownership can be determined from the parents. Royal swans were left unmarked in the 20th century and any unmarked wild mute swans are property of the Crown. The only other permitted owners are the Worshipful Companies of Vintners and Dyers. Vintners' swans have a nick cut on each side of the bill and Dyers on one side. Their ancient marks were more complex, as below, when there were numerous permitted owners.

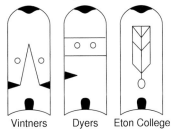

Vintners   Dyers   Eton College

Mute swans appear to have had royal status since the 12th century. By 1378 there was a Keeper of the King's Swans.   *Swan Upping* Pam Marson & Gordon Cullingham *Windlesora* Vol 1 5pp

19 Boulter's Lock and Cookham

About 9 km/5¾ miles with an extension of 1¼ km/¾ mile; farmland and Thames Path with ¾ mile of residential roads. OS maps 1:25000 172 Chiltern Hills East 1:50000 175 Reading.

Start: Boulter's Lock car park (pay & display) SU 902 825 or the Moor car park at Cookham, SU 892 853, or Blackmoor Lane, SU 892 823.

Kings Arms 01628 530667
The Crown 01628 520163
The Ferry 01628 525123
Bel & the Dragon
01628 521263

Linking walks
8✪ 18★

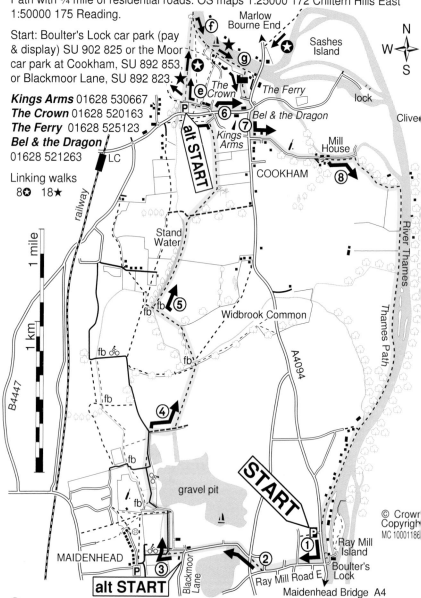

© Crown
Copyright
MC 10001186

① From the car park go along the river bank to Boulter's Lock and the bridge from Ray Mill Island (200m). Turn R along Ray Mill Road East through Maidenhead (450m).

② Just after the Pagoda side road R bear R on the path between gardens to the next road (100m). Cross and go along Summerleaze Road to the end (500m).

38

③ At the bend stay ahead on the footpath to the meadow (100m). Near the footbridge turn R on the cycle track (300m). At the tarmac drive go L almost to the bridge (100m) then R on the cycle track to the T-junction (300m). Cross the R corner of the next field and go on along more cycle track (250m).

④ Take the side track R beside the fence (Green Way East)(200m) then turn L on the path over the field to the tree-lined edge (450m).

On the hilltop far R is Cliveden. Go on into the meadow (Widbrook Common), over the brook, ahead near the L edge to the next corner (250m) and ½L over the field to the corner near a footbridge (250m).

⑤ Turn R along the edge of the field and stay ahead all the way to Cookham: beside Strand Water, round bends, obliquely over the farm track in the trees (700m), round a L bend (250m), and soon between gardens to the end near Moor Place (450m). Turn R to the road junction and war memorial opposite the **Crown** (50m). ★✪

ⓔ *Extension of 1¼ km/¾ mile through Cookham Meadows: Cross to the **Crown** (50m) and go L at the edge of the green (200m). From the Moor car park enter the meadow and continue on the path ahead to the river (550m).*

ⓕ *Return along the river (500m).*

ⓖ *Pass R through the churchyard to the main road (250m) and R round the bends (100m).* ➤⑦

⑥ Walk through Cookham, R, past Stanley Spencer's house R and the **Kings Arms** R to the **Bel & the Dragon** L (300m). Turn R.

⑦ Follow the main road, A4094, towards Maidenhead (200m) and turn L on Mill Lane. Stay ahead on the winding lane until past the Mill House L (600m).

⑧ Just after the Mill House, join the path R of the drive and carry on beside it (200m) then turn R to the river (400m) and R along the Thames Path. Opposite, the 2nd house is Spring Cottage (300m). Keep on until the path joins the road in Maidenhead (2000m) and a bit further to the car park (50m).

Sashes Island opposite Cookham was SCEAFTESEGE in the "Buhral Hideage" written c 915. Burhs were fortified enclosures. They were set up by Alfred the Great or his son, Edward the Elder, as barracks for a standing army to counter the predations of the Vikings. There were 27 in the kingdom of Wessex and others appeared later in the rump of Mercia not held by the Danes. Some buhrs gave rise to new towns hence *borough*. The Thames was a major highway for the invaders who took Reading in 871 and received a fleet later in the year. Weapons have been dredged up near the island. The alignment of the Roman road between St Albans and Silchester suggests it crossed the Thames via the island.

Spring Cottage in the grounds of Cliveden is where Christine Keeler got to know Yevgeny Ivanov and John Profumo in 1961. The tenant, Stephen Ward, Viscount Astor's osteopath and friend, manipulated bones, people and events and tried to effect a rapprochement between the USSR and the West in the Cold War. A disillusioned lover of Christine Keeler fired a gun at Ward's London house in 1963, bringing him to the attention of the police and her to the attention of the press. Her stories put Profumo in the spotlight; "*he would, wouldn't he*" was Mandy Rice Davies' rejoinder to what Viscount Astor said in court. Profumo (Hobson's choice) resigned from the government, having lied to Parliament; Ward killed himself.

20 Bray, Maidenhead and the Thames

About 8¾ km/5½ miles with a zigzag through Bray village; flat apart from the steps at the bridges, no stiles, little shade; less pleasant stretches beside major roads. The extension of 1½ km/1 mile is along the Thames past Monkey Island
OS maps 1:25000 160 Windsor + 172 Chiltern Hills East, 1:50000 175 Reading.

Start at Bray from the main village car park, SU 903 794 or the smaller car park at the other end of the village or at Bray Wick Park car park, SU 894 794.
On the extension, Bray Lake car park, SU 912 786, is near the route.

Linking 20✳ 22❖ 40✿   Maidenhead High Street has many eating places

The Hinds Head ☎ 01628 626151
The Crown ☎ 01628 621936

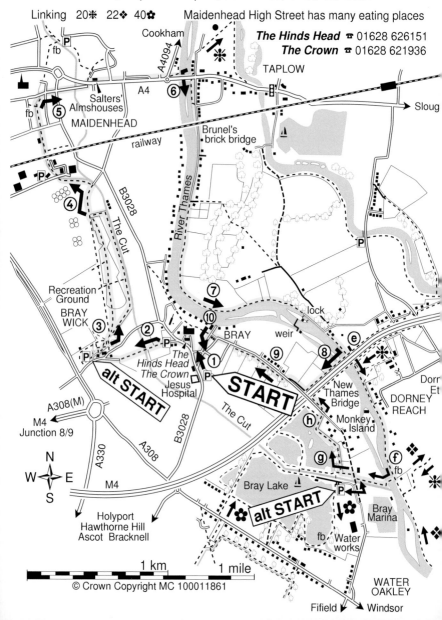

① From the car park in Bray cross the road to see Jesus Hospital then walk into the village past the **Crown**. Fork R of the **Hind's Head** under the arch to the churchyard (300m) then turn L to the street (50m) and R to the grass (30m).

② Go L through the car park and along the tarmac footpath between fields and over the Cut. At the end (400m) go on up the lane (100m) and L up the road (100m). Cross into Bray Wick Park R.

③ From the vehicle entrance follow the tarmac R along the edge near the buildings (60m). When the path bends L, stay ahead down the slope and over the footbridge between ponds to the path junction at the track from the road (100m). Continue on the level hard track, almost ahead, over the bridge (50m) and fork R. Either go up the steps L and along the mound of reconstituted land (850m) or stay on the tarmac path which soon runs beside the Cut (850m) then bends L to the main track (150m).

④ After the mound continue on the main track round a R curve to the Cut (200m). Don't cross but turn L on the path L of the water to the next road (300m). Cross the bridge and continue on the R side of the ditch, under the London-Bristol railway (200m) and over a road (200m). Stay ahead through Maidenhead to the end of the footpath at High Street (200m).

⑤ Walk R along High Street, over crossroads and along Moorbridge Road to the closed end (400m). Go under or over the main road to the Salters' Almshouses and on L of the main road, the A4 (650m).

Pause in the riverside gardens to view Maidenhead Bridge then cross (200m). From the bridge, Taplow Court is visible on the hilltop L. ✳

⑥ Turn into Mill Lane L (10m) and L through the boatyard and under Maidenhead Bridge to the end of the path (200m). Continue on the little road under the railway bridge (Sounding Arch) to the end of the houses (650m) then on the path passing opposite Bray Church, on the other side (800m).

⑦ Continue on the Thames Path past Bray Lock (650m) to the New Thames Bridge (M4) (400m).

ⓔ *Extension of 1½ km/1 mile: Stay on the river bank under the bridge past Monkey Island and the Dorney Reach houses to Summerleaze footbridge R (900m).* ❖

ⓕ *Cross the river and carry on beside The Cut to the cart bridge over the channel (400m).* ✿

ⓖ *Don't cross it but turn R (40m) and take the footpath L between fences (100m). Turn R on the 1st side path (200m). After the field R the path bends L past houses (150m) then R to the road (150m).*

ⓗ Walk L on the road up over the motorway and down (450m). ➜⑨

⑧ Cross the motorway bridge on the near side and go on past fields (400m) then turn R, beside the embankment, to the road (150m).

⑨ Carry on into Bray village; a path L under trees offers summer shade (600m). When the road bends L stay ahead in front of the timber framed houses (50m) and turn R to the river slipway (70m).

⑩ Walk back along Ferry Road to the X-junction (200m) then bear L to the village car park (200m).

21 Taplow, Jubilee River and Thames

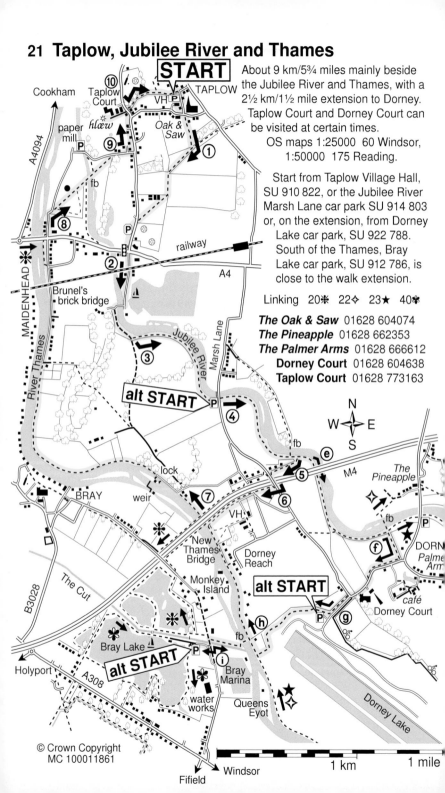

START

About 9 km/5¾ miles mainly beside the Jubilee River and Thames, with a 2½ km/1½ mile extension to Dorney. Taplow Court and Dorney Court can be visited at certain times.

OS maps 1:25000 60 Windsor,
1:50000 175 Reading.

Start from Taplow Village Hall, SU 910 822, or the Jubilee River Marsh Lane car park SU 914 803 or, on the extension, from Dorney Lake car park, SU 922 788. South of the Thames, Bray Lake car park, SU 912 786, is close to the walk extension.

Linking 20❋ 22◇ 23★ 40❋

The Oak & Saw 01628 604074
The Pineapple 01628 662353
The Palmer Arms 01628 666612
Dorney Court 01628 604638
Taplow Court 01628 773163

Cookham

Taplow Court

paper mill

hlæw

Oak & Saw

TAPLOW

VH

fb

railway

A4

MAIDENHEAD

Brunel's brick bridge

Jubilee River

Marsh Lane

alt START

lock

BRAY

weir

New Thames Bridge

Dorney Reach

Monkey Island

VH

The Pineapple

M4

DORN
Palme
Arm

café

Dorney Court

alt START

B3028

The Cut

Bray Lake

alt START

Holyport

A308

water works

Bray Marina

Queens Eyot

Dorney Lake

© Crown Copyright
MC 100011861

Windsor

Fifield

1 km   1 mile

(i) *If starting at Bray Lake car park walk back along the drive to the bend (100m). Go through the gate to the track, L over the bridge (25m), R beside The Cut (200m) and over the Thames.* ➤(h)

① At Taplow village walk down to the church and **Oak & Saw** (200m). and take the footpath opposite the T-junction (200m). Emerging from between hedges, bear R on the main path between fields (400m). On entering the field near the farm, cross diagonally R and descend to the furthest corner (250m). Walk down the road L (250m).

② Cross the A4 and go along the lane opposite under the London to Bristol railway (100m), past the Taplow Lake Sailing Club, R over the Jubilee River (350m) and L on the track beside it (250m).

③ When the river curves L, turn L along the side track beside it. Keep on to the next road (1000m).

④ From the car park go over the road and on along the river past the next footbridge (800m).

(e) *Extension of 2½ km/1½ miles into Dorney: continue ahead under the M4 (200m) to the next river footbridge (900m).* ✧★

(f) *Turn R on the cross path from the footbridge, along the end of the field (200m) then follow the path R beside the minor road Court Lane, past Dorney Court and the church L (300m). When the road bends R (100m) stay ahead on the path R of the access road of Dorney Lake (200m).*

(g) *Before the car park and lake, bear R on the winding path outside the fields and keep on to the River*

Thames (800m). Turn R to Summerleaze footbridge (100m).

(i) *If returning to Bray Lake car park cross the river.* ✳✳   *If not:*

(h) *Follow the tow path upstream past Monkey Island and the houses of Dorney Reach to the motorway bridge (900m).* ✳ ➤⑦

⑤ Soon after the footbridge (50m), turn back R on the side path near houses (300m) then L up the zigzag path to the road (100m).

⑥ Turn L over the bridge (80m) then zigzag down R. Stay near the motorway. At the road follow the drive to the sports field and cross the grass ahead to the Thames (500m). ✳ Turn R.

⑦ Stay ahead beside the river past Bray Lock (400m), past Bray church opposite (700m), along the tarmac lane with houses (800m) and under the Sounding Arch (500m) to the side road (150m). Drop to the river bank and carry on under Maidenhead Bridge (200m) to the minor road R (40m).

⑧ Go L on the minor road (150m). After the S-bend diverge R on the path over the Jubilee River (300m). Go up the slope (250m) then R to the end of the lane (250m).

⑨ Walk up the road L, round the bends until opposite the footpath in the trees just after the last house R (350m). (You can go along the drive L to see the Tæppa Hlœw and/or stay ahead (50m) to the next drive for a view of Taplow Court).

⑩ Cross to the footpath under the trees. Stay on this path, behind gardens (400m) then turn R, down the road towards Taplow Church and village green (150m) with steps to the village hall car park R.

22 Boveney, Dorney and the Thames

About 8¼ km/5 miles beside the Thames and Jubilee River with extensions of ¾ km/½ mile and 1 km/¾ mile; good in winter; level apart from the footbridge over the Thames. Dorney Court can be visited on certain afternoons and could be the starting point. OS maps 1:25000 60 Windsor, 1:50000 175 Reading.

Start from Boveney car park, SU 938 777 or the car park at the NW end of Dorney Lake, SU 920 788. On the south side of the Thames, Bray Lake car park, SU 912 786, is fairly close to the walk route. Close to the extension there is a Jubilee River car park near the *Pineapple*, SU 928 795.

Dorney Court Kitchen Garden Café ☎ 01628 669999   Linking walks 20❖
The Pineapple ☎ 01628 662353   21✦ 23★ 24☆ 40❀
The Palmer Arms ☎ 01628 666612
Dorney Court ☎ 01628 604638

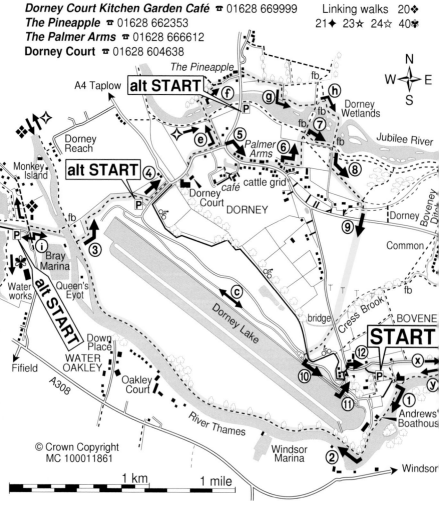

ⓘ *If starting at Bray Lake car park walk back along the drive to the bend (100m). Go through the gate to the track, L over the cart bridge (50m), R beside the Cut (200m) and over Summerleaze (Thames) footbridge.* ✧ *Follow the tow path R, downstream (100m).* ➛③

44

① At Boveney car park take the footpath from the end opposite the vehicle entrance (50m). Turn R on the path beside the field and the church (100m) then R along the Thames Path past the large shed (boathouse) (250m) (where paths R link to Dorney Lake). Go on round the bend in the river (200m).

② Keep on along the river bank. On the opposite bank are Windsor Marina (750m), Oakley Court (with tower) (900m), Down Place (large white house) (500m) and the Bray Marina café (800m). ❖◇❀

ⓘ *If returning to Bray Lake stay ahead to the footbridge (100m).*

③ Opposite the marina café follow the side path, which winds to the drive from Dorney Lake (800m).

④ Follow the drive L to the road (200m). Stay ahead on the path L of the road past Dorney Church (100m) and round a curve to the Kitchen Garden drive R (250m), which gives a good view of Dorney Court and access to the café. Keep on to the end of the road (60m).

ⓔ *Extension of ¾ km/½ mile via the **Pineapple**: Take the path L at the end of the field (200m) and cross the Jubilee River to the path in the trees (150m).*

ⓕ *Turn R. Continue on the farm track then lane to the road (350m). Opposite the Pineapple, between the houses, take the path in the field, converging on the R edge (150m). Cross to the adjacent field and follow the L edge (150m).*

ⓖ *Turn R along the end hedge to the river (200m) then L along the bank and over the track from the first footbridge (300m).*

ⓗ *Bear L up the slope (50m) and turn R towards the next bridge via the track above the wetlands. Re-cross the river (300m). ☆★ ✦⑧*

⑤ Go R on the pavement through Dorney village past the **Palmer Arms** (300m) and ahead almost to the next side road L (150m).

⑥ Just before the side road take the footpath L between the gardens to the field (70m). Turn R along the edge (100m) then L across the field (200m). Keep on ahead to the Jubilee River (50m).

⑦ Go R along the bank above the Dorney Wetlands to the next footbridge (200m). Turn R. ☆

⑧ Follow the track away from the bridge (150m). Before the gate bear L on the oblique cross path from the field R. Stay ahead to the gate R to Dorney Common (400m).

⑨ Walk across the grass and the road (no path). Aim for the furthest corner of the Common between trees L and houses R and cross the little road bridge (800m). Bear R on the path into the corner of the Common (300m) and pass through the boundary gate to Dorney Rowing Lake (60m).

⑩ Walk L along the lake but avoid the tarmac edge if rowing coaches are using it (300m).

⑪ At the first house L take the drive L past the houses (100m) and ⑫ follow the road R to the Boveney car park entrance (150m).

ⓧ *Extension of 1 km/¾ mile to Boveney Lock: Keep on along the lane to the River Thames (700m).*

ⓨ *Turn R along the lock and stay beside the river (800m). After the church go R to the car park (150m).*

23 Clewer Church to Dorney Wetlands

About 8½ km/5¼ miles; two extensions to Dorney Lake and the wetlands, each of 1½ km/1 mile: mostly flat; no stiles; little summer shade; good in winter and for birdwatching. OS maps 1:25000 160 Windsor, 1:50000 175 Reading.

Start at the Leisure Centre pay & display car park in Windsor. After 2pm roadside parking is permitted near Clewer Church, SU 956 771. Near the extension there is a car park in Boveney, SU 938 777.

Linking walks 21★ 22★ 24✳ 25○

The Palmer Arms in Dorney ☎ 01628 666612

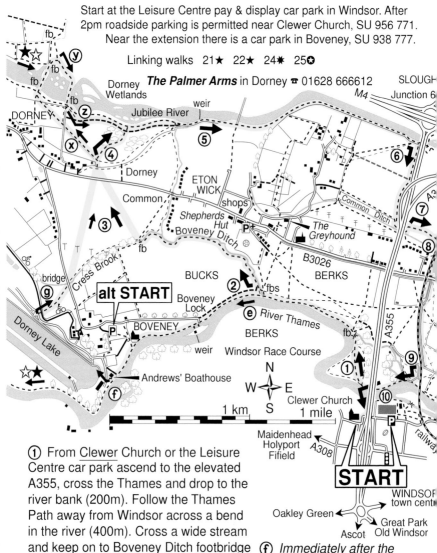

① From Clewer Church or the Leisure Centre car park ascend to the elevated A355, cross the Thames and drop to the river bank (200m). Follow the Thames Path away from Windsor across a bend in the river (400m). Cross a wide stream and keep on to Boveney Ditch footbridge (opposite Eton Wick far R) (750m).

ⓔ *Extension of 1½ km/1 mile to Dorney Lake: Stay beside the river through Boveney Lock (550m), past the church at Boveney (500m) and round the curve to a large shed (boathouse) (300m). ★☆*

ⓕ *Immediately after the boathouse turn R on the path and cross to Dorney Lake (100m). Walk along the grassy mound R of the lake to where the road bends close to the lake (600m).*

46

(g) *Halfway to the next link road (30m) find the path through the fence R and follow it across the cycle track to the large expanse of grass which is Dorney Common (50m). Aim over the grass for the little low bridge where the lane crosses the Cress Brook (300m). Cross the bridge.* ✦③

② Turn R (30m). Cross the next footbridge (into Buckinghamshire) then follow the edge of the field L of Boveney Ditch behind the houses of Eton Wick (800m) and along the side stream to the next public footbridge R (200m). Cross to the grass of Dorney Common.

③ Identify the hillock beyond the road ahead and the farm buildings near it at the edge of Dorney. Aim for the gate in the hedge just R of the farm buildings (700m). Pass through to the path junction (30m).

(x) *Extension of 1½ km/1 mile to Dorney Wetlands. Bear L on the flat path diverging from the line of buildings (350m). Cross the farm road and the next field in the same oblique line (250m). Keep on over the Jubilee River and another (short) footbridge (300m).*

(y) *Turn up the first side track R (50m). Curve R down to the next footbridge and re-cross (300m).*

(z) *Turn L but diverge up to the higher parallel track rising over the mound past a view point. Keep on to the weir (1000m).* ✦⑤

④ Bear R up the path over the top of the hillock and down to the edge of the wetlands (300m). Turn R along the river to the weir (500m).

⑤ Continue along the Jubilee River past a farm bridge (400m) to the major road bridge (1400m). ✪✱

⑥ Turn R along the path beside the road embankment (600m).

⑦ At the ditch, turn L under the road and keep to the track curving away from the ditch then parallel with it (400m). ✪✱

⑧ Pass under the railway and turn R beside it. ✱ Keep on to the next road (250m). Cross (30m L) to the tarmac path at the edge of the field and continue ahead (600m).

⑨ At the tarmac lane go under the railway but continue beside it, soon curving R to the Thames (150m). Turn R along the bank (300m).

⑩ For Clewer Church pass under the bridge then cross (300m).

Dorney Common is doubly unusual: it retains its ancient style of regulation and appears to be good arable land. Crops were grown during the Second World War. Most surviving common land is no good for arable. Following is a small extract of the regulations:

Scale for calculating stint

Total commons shall be 198 neat beasts & 77 horses. Commonable cottage without agricultural land 1 cow and 1 youngling bullock. Every 5 acres above the first five acres up to a total of 70, add 1 neat beast. Geese - 1 goose and 1 gander to each Commoner and no more. Hogs - double the number of neat beasts. Commoners may put their hogs on the Commons of this manor from 1 Nov until 28 Feb. All pigs shall be deemed as hogs which shall be pigged before 1 May, but all pigged after that date shall not be... hogs. No Commoner shall pasture sick, diseased, infectious or distempered animals .... on pain of forfeiture To the Lord of £5; To the Hayward 5/- when pounded. Commoners shall not exceed their stints of ... common rights except that they may let or take their commons from one another at the best price and advantage at a Market of Rights... at which the Hayward shall be present. The Commons of this Manor shall be open from the 1st April until the 31st October.

24 Clewer, Eton Wick and Eton

About 6½ km/4 miles with an extension of 2 km/1¼ miles along the Jubilee River; level apart from the bridge over the Thames; good in winter; stiles only on the extension. OS maps 1:25000 160 Windsor, 1:50000 175 Reading.

Start at Eton Wick car park, SU 948 784, or the Leisure Centre pay & display car park in Windsor. After 2pm roadside parking is permitted near Clewer Church, SU 956 771. On the extension use the Jubilee River car park, SU 970 788.

The Shepherds Hut ☎ 01753 868644   **The Greyhound** ☎ 01753 868633
Three Horseshoes ☎ 01753 867889   **Watermans Arms** ☎ 01753 861001

Linking walks 22☆ 23✱ 25❃

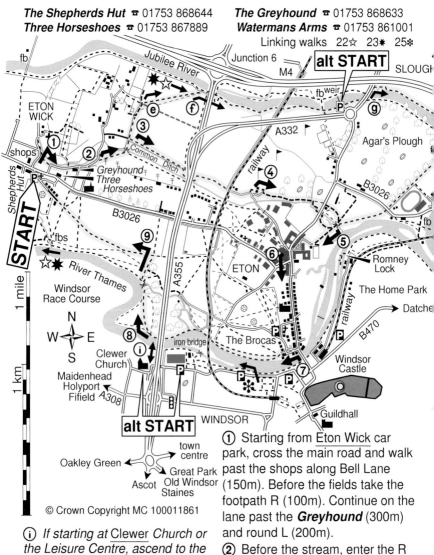

© Crown Copyright MC 100011861

(i) *If starting at Clewer Church or the Leisure Centre, ascend to the A355 (100m) and cross the river (200m). Drop to the river bank and and walk away from Windsor.* ➔(8)

(1) Starting from Eton Wick car park, cross the main road and walk past the shops along Bell Lane (150m). Before the fields take the footpath R (100m). Continue on the lane past the *Greyhound* (300m) and round L (200m).

(2) Before the stream, enter the R field and converge L on the stream to the footbridge (200m). Cross the bridge and the next field (60m).

48

ⓔ *Extension of 2 km/1¼ mile via the Jubilee River: Stay ahead at the L edge of the field and along the track from the farm to the diagonal path R (250m). This path often starts before the cross-field track but officially starts at it. Cross the field converging on the M4 towards the corner of the field as seen between the roads (450m).*

ⓕ *Join the track beside the* Jubilee River. *Go under the road and on, under the railway (600m) to the next road bridge (500m).*

ⓖ *Cross the road and turn L over the bridge (100m). Take the path R after the trees. Go on near the river almost to the houses at The Myrke (750m).*✻

ⓗ *Cross the footbridge and continue along the track through the Eton sports field (600m), over the road and ahead to the Playing Fields brick footbridge (400m).* ➧⑤

③ Turn R parallel with the stream, (500m). At the major road the track bends R to pass under the bridge then L to the original direction. Carry on under the railway (250m) and along the lane (150m).

④ On the curve turn L on the side lane to the cottages and continue on the track along the sports fields until it bends R after a cart bridge (500m). The right-of-way is ahead over the grass to the gate in the fence (100m), across the road and past the lodge to the brick foot-bridge but most walkers stay on the track (no RoW) R,L,R over another cart bridge, under the road (100m) and round R,L (200m).

⑤ From the brick footbridge make for Eton College (150m). At the buildings continue on the tarmac drive R then L through the arch and ahead to the road (150m).

⑥ Turn L. Walk along Eton High Street which has several cafés and pubs. Keep on to the river but stop on Windsor Bridge (600m). ✻

⑦ Return from the bridge and turn along Brocas Street. Pass L of the ***Watermans Arms*** to the Brocas (meadow) (150m). Follow the river to the next road bridge (1100m).

ⓘ *If finishing at Clewer Church pass under the bridge then cross.*

⑧ Keep to the Thames Path over the bend in the river (400m). ☆✱

⑨ After the side stream, turn R on the side path (200m). Disregard the track R between fields but turn L on the cross path from the road arches. Keep to the main path towards Eton Wick (1000m) and along the edge of the football field to the car park and shops (300m). The ***Shepherds Hut*** is L (100m) and the ***Horseshoes*** is R (100m).

The **Brocas** is the meadow beside the Thames at Eton. Presumably it was owned or donated by the Brocas family perhaps to endow the Clewer chantry. The family were Gascons who had come to England in Henry II's service. Early medieval English kings were also Dukes of Gascony. English soldiers and royal officials served in Gascony and Gascons served in Britain. Arnald de Brocas was killed in 1314 during the Scottish wars of Edward II. Sir Bernard Brocas, a friend of the Black Prince and William of Wyckham, fought at Poitiers and Crécy and survived to be Captain of Calais. It was he who founded the chantry at Clewer Church in 1384, ten years before he died. His family home was Beaurépair near Basingstoke after he married the heiress. The number of estates with the Brocas name round the country suggest they were a virile lot. *The Brocas Family* Windlesora No 3

25 Clewer, Eton, the Jubilee River and Windsor

About 8 km/5 miles with an extension of ¾ km/½ mile and a short cut of 1 km/ ¾ mile; level apart from bridge steps; no stiles. The extension is uphill to the castle. Good in winter. OS maps 1:25000 160 Windsor, 1:50000 175 Reading.

Park at Windsor Leisure Centre (pay & display). After 2pm roadside parking is permitted near Clewer Church, SU 956 771.

Linking walks 23❂ 24✽ 26★

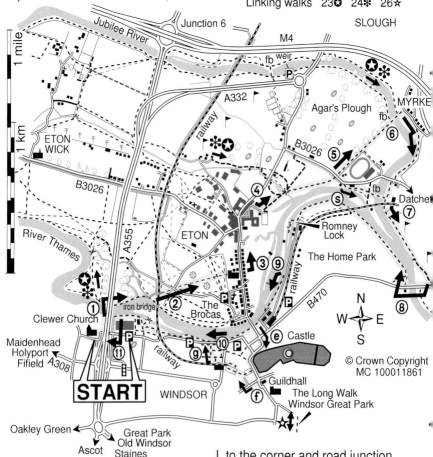

① Starting at the Leisure Centre or Clewer Church, ascend to the A355 bridge (100m) and cross the river (200m). Drop to the river bank ❂☆ and follow the Thames Path towards Windsor Castle (300m).

② After the 2nd footbridge fork L (50m). When the main path curves L, turn R under the railway (GWR) and cross the small field diagonally

L to the corner and road junction (100m). Cross the larger lane into the football fields and aim straight for Eton Church (400m) or skirt round the pitches. Pass L of the church to Eton High Street (200m).

③ Go L along the street past Eton Chapel and the Eton Wick side road (300m) to the bend (100m).

④ Opposite Common Lane L, pass through the arched gateway

50

in the Eton College wall and walk along the drive past the buildings (permitted path)(150m). Outside the next archway turn R (60m) then L on the gravel track through the playing fields (250m). After the brick footbridge bear R, parallel with the river, to the road (400m).

Ⓢ *Short cut of 1 km/¾ mile: Turn R along the road (100m) and R on the drive after the house. Go past Masters' Boathouse. Follow the main path and cross the Jubilee River (350m). Turn R.* ➜Ⓖ

⑤ Cross the road and continue on the straight track beside the sports fields and over the Jubilee River to The Myrke (600m).

⑥ Walk R along the road almost to the end of the houses (150m) then take the footpath R which follows the Jubilee River round to the next road (400m). Cross and carry on beside the river passing the end of the footbridge (200m).

⑦ Go under the railway (L&SWR) (50m) and keep on at the R edge of Datchet Golf Course (450m), continuing on a cart track (200m).

⑧ Just before the track bends to the road take the footpath R and walk back along the road over Victoria Bridge (200m). As soon as possible after the bridge, drop R to the river and follow the bank to the railway (Thames Path) (650m). Go under the arch and continue beside the river to the boatyard (500m). To see Romney Lock go through the gate R. Carry on along the lane from the boatyard (500m).

⑨ Near the railway footbridge L diverge R of the car park on the footpath and stay at the riverside to Windsor Bridge (450m).

ⓔ *Extension of ¾ km/½ mile into Windsor: Go L on the road from the bridge up round the castle wall to the first crossroads (500m).* ★

ⓕ *Turn R down Peascod Street (100m) then R along the passage, Goswell Hill (100m). Turn L to the station canopy then R into the building. Pass R of the railway line to the end of the platform (200m).*

ⓖ *Go over the footbridge & down the stair-tower. Follow paths over the public gardens (200m).* ➜⑩

⑩ Cross the road and drop to the river bank. Stay on the tarmac path nearest the river under the brick railway bridge (800m or 400m) and on to the large road bridge (300m).

⑪ Turn L up the slipway road (150m) then L to the Leisure Centre or R to Clewer Church.

x 2

Scurvy grass has invaded main roads in recent years to form a 6 inch fringe - mauve or white - when flowering in April. It is a halophyte,"salt-plant", that lives close to sea beaches and is able to exploit the zone sprayed with road salt. The plants may not need salt but can survive where others fail. Mowing of verges also favours them because they keep their heads down. They are several species of *Cochlearia*. In the south of England the white flowered species is *C. officinalis* and the lilac is *C. danica*. They are not grasses but in the family Brassicaceæ. Like the other edible plants of this family, watercress rocket and cabbage, they are rich in ascorbic acid (Vitamin C). It is said mariners ate them to cure scurvy.

26 Windsor Great Park - North

Newcomers to the Great Park should read the WGP box at the back of the book. About 8¼ km/5¼ miles with an extension of ¾ km/½ mile. Grass, hard paths and park roads, mainly in the deer enclosure; optional shade; good for picnics; dogs have to be on leads. OS maps 1:25000 160 Windsor, 1:50000 175 Reading.

Start from the parking area east of Sheet Street Road, SU 962 744, near Windsor or the little car park opposite Ranger's Gate, SU 953 734, or the parking layby outside Bishops Gate, SU 979 722.

Linking walks   25★ 27✻ 27✻

The Fox & Hounds
☎ 01753 433098
The Oxford Blue
☎ 01753 861954
The Union Inn
☎ 01753 861955

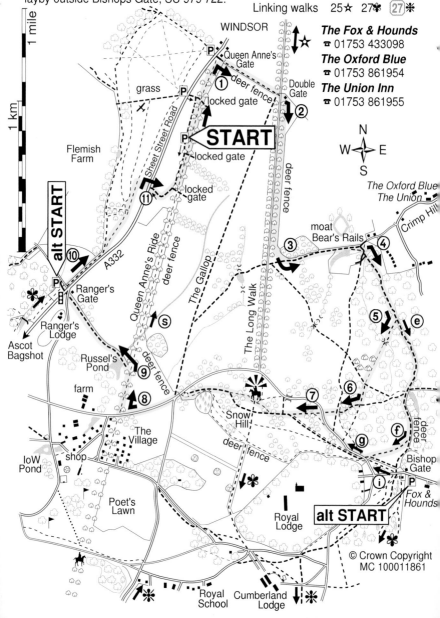

© Crown Copyright
MC 100011861

(i) *If starting from Bishops Gate follow the diverging path R of the road beside the <u>deer fence</u> and go through the gate (250m).* ➤(g)

(1) From the parking area near Windsor, cross to the path near the deer fence and turn L to the corner (600m). Turn R along the footpath outside the deer fence (450m). ★

(2) Near the Long Walk (tarmac) enter the deer fence R. Walk along the tarmac drive or over the grass beside the L fence (1000m)

(3) When the fence bends L go round the wood 90° and on along the track, past the pond R, almost to Bear Rails Gate (600m).

(4) Before the houses turn R on the main track into the wood (50m). Over the stream, fork L up to the brow of the hill (300m). Keep to the track, watching out for the minor side path R (to the grass visible outside the wood) at the start of the parallel R side ditch (250m).

(e) *Extension of ¾ km/½ mile near Bishops Gate: Keep to the track ahead (500m) past side tracks L&R, the pond L and up (350m).*

(f) *Take the diverging path R up round the edge of the wood to the tarmac park road near the deer fence gate (350m).* ❀❈
*(For Bishops Gate and the **Fox & Hounds** turn L outside the fence.)*

(g) *Carry on along the road past the belt of trees up L (300m) to the cross path at the start of the next L curve (170m). Ascend L.* ➤(7)

(5) Take the side path through the trees down over a little bridge to open grass (150m). Go straight up the slope, L of clumps of trees, to the gap in the wood (300m). Cross the track along the edge and go up

through the trees to the cross path with twin ditches (150m).

(6) Turn R on this path up to the edge of the wood (150m) and ahead to the tarmac road (100m). Cross and carry on up.

(7) Pass between trees and over the rise to the junction of tracks in the dip above the bridge R (300m). Carry on up beside the horse track ahead (100m) and take the first side path R to the Copper Horse on the top of Snow Hill (100m). ❀

Northwards is <u>Windsor Castle</u> with Slough beyond it. To the right of it are the Queen Mother Reservoir, the arch of Wembley Stadium and the Shard.

Continue in the same direction (ie the way the statue is facing) through more trees, over the grass and into trees again near the deer fence (200m). Keep to the fence ahead down to the gate (200m). Outside, fork R down the road to Queen Ann's Ride, the crossing avenue of trees with the millstone and The Village above L (450m).

(8) Turn R down the middle (300m).
(9) Watch out for the diverging track to Russels Pond through the trees. Go L on it past the pond and over the rise to Ranger's Gate (700m). Cross Sheet Street Road (A332) to the <u>Flemish Farm</u> drive.

(10) Follow the path down between the field and the A332 (350m). After the hedge and main path bend away from the road, branch R on one of the minor paths over the rise parallel with the road. Keep on until opposite the track from the parking places on the other side of the road (600m).

(11) Cross to it and carry on to the parking place (400m).

27 Windsor Great Park - Middle

Newcomers to the Great Park should read the WGP box at the back of the book. About 9 km/5½ miles with an extension of 1¾ km/1½ mile and a short cut of 2¼ km/1½ miles; grass and Park roads; no stiles; gently undulating; dogs on leads; good for picnics. OS Maps 1:25000 160 Windsor, 1:50000 175 Reading.

Start at the car park opposite Cranbourne Gate, SU 947 727 (on brow of hill), or the car park opposite Rangers Gate, SU 953 734, or the layby at Bishops Gate, SU 979 722.

Linking walks 26❀ [27] ★ [28] ☀

The Fox & Hounds 01784 433098
Savill Garden Restaurant 01784 485402

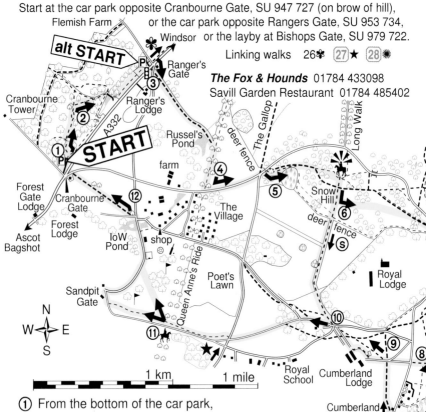

© Crown Copyright
MC 100011861

① From the bottom of the car park, go through the gate to Cranbourne Wood and ahead briefly (40m). Bear L (50m) then R on the path into the little valley in the trees (50m). Up the other side (20m), turn R on the path (N) (250m).

② Take the path R (or, if missed, the path beside the next fence) to the gates at Pickle Herring Pond (250m). Take the track just over the outlet (40m) then bear L under trees to the grass (50m). Keep on near the A332 hedge to the drive of Flemish Farm & car park (300m). ❀

③ Cross the main road. Up the drive from Rangers Gate (50m) go up the track R of the lodge over the rise and down past Russells Pond to Queen Ann's Drive, the grassy avenue (650m). Walk up the avenue R to the park road (300m).

④ Turn L on the park road (450m).
⑤ Inside the deer fence turn R up the footpath R of the horse track (200m). When the R fence curves

R, keep on beside the horse track (150m). When that bends R in the trees, stay ahead on the footpath along the top of Snow Hill and out to the Copper Horse (200m). Turn R across the hilltop over the horse track to the north brow (150m). Royal Lodge Windsor is ½L below.

Ⓢ *Short cut of 2¼ km/1½ miles: Continue straight down through the the deer fence (150m), between fields (500m), under trees around the fence of Royal Lodge and up to the road (150m). Turn R.* ➜Ⓘ⓪

⑥ Turn L over the grass, outside the trees, eventually converging on the horse track. Carry on beside it down to the road (850m). Go through the deer fence gates (50m) and on beside the deer fence to Bishops Gate (250m). (The **Fox & Hounds** is 150m outside.)

⑦ Take the path along the edge of the lodge garden and stay on it round a R bend (250m). Watch out for the side path R to the Cow Pond (500m). Cross to the edge of the pond (40m). ★

ⓔ *Extension 1¾ km/1 mile: Turn L to the corner (80m), re-join the major path L and carry on (R) down to the tarmac drive (400m). Continue (L) on the drive passing between the Savill Garden entrance and car park (400m). Stay ahead on the tarmac path (150m).* ✳

ⓕ *When the side path bends R around the corner of the Savill Garden fence, continue up the knoll past the obelisk and down to the pond (150m) then turn R along the edge to the main path. Carry on outside the Savill Garden fence, over the bridge (250m) and beside Smith's Lawn to the road (600m).*★

Ⓖ *Cross the grass slightly L to the horse track on the other side.* Go R, round the L bend behind the house and on until the track crosses a road (350m). Turn L. ➜Ⓖ

⑧ Identify the broad path in the trees opposite and go round to it, L (250m) or R (400m). Walk away from the pond, past labelled oaks R, (250m), over the road and on to the next tarmac junction (200m).

⑨ Keep on to the entrance of Cumberland Lodge (130m). Turn R on the path outside the hedge past the tennis court round to the back drive (150m). Walk along the drive R out to the park road (200m).

⑩ Follow the road L past a side road and drive, down out of the trees and on to crossroads (750m). Stay ahead on the road or the path R of it to the Elizabeth II equestrian statue at Queen Anns Ride (450m).

⑪ After this it is best to cut ½R across the golf course to the next road (400m) but if golfers are playing, continue with the road to the lodge at Sandpit Gate (see the kennels) (550m) then turn back R on the other road (350m). Follow the road past the York Club R and Isle of White Pond L (350m).

⑫ From the next drive L take the diverging horse track up the grass slope to pass R of the hedge at Cranbourne Gate lodge (550m). Cross the road to the Cranbourne Tower drive and car park (100m).

28 Marsh Lock, Henley Bridge and Harpsden

About 8½ km/5¼ miles; the Thames, undulating farmland and woods with an extension of 1¼ km/¾ mile to Upper Bolney. OS maps 1:25000 159 Reading +171 Chiltern Hills W, 1:50000 175 Reading.

Start from Mill Lane car park in Henley, SU 770 817, or from Harpsden Church, SU 763 809, or from one of the roadside parking spots in Harpsden Wood.

Linking walks 1✴ 11☆ 29❁

Baskerville Arms
0118 940 3332

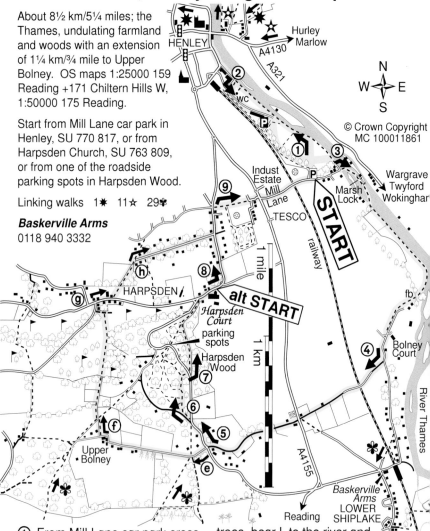

© Crown Copyright
MC 100011861

① From Mill Lane car park cross the meadow ½L to the river (250m) and carry on beside the Thames to Henley Bridge (1000m). ✴☆

② Return the same way until level with the island (350m) then turn R into the public gardens and make your way along them to the Rowing Museum R (300m). Carry on along the drive then the R edge of the meadows (500m). Before the end trees, bear L to the river and pass the trees to Mill Lane (300m).

③ From the end of Mill Lane go over the river on the towpath bridge to Marsh Lock (200m) and ahead back to the river bank (150m). Continue (L) on the Thames Path round a R bend in the river (900m). After the footbridge, at the houses, carry on along the winding drive past Bolney Court L (350m). ❁

56

④ Soon after the Bolney Court gate (50m) turn R on the Chilterns Way byway, up over the railway and on (750m). Continue over the A4155 up to the next road (850m).

ⓔ *Extension of 1¼ km/¾ mile to Upper Bolney & Harpsden village: Cross the road and go along the private road opposite, round a slight bend (100m) and straight on, to Upper Bolney House (650m). Pass round R and L bends.*

ⓕ *After the L bend (50m) take the footpath R between the garden and field to the cross path (100m). Cross to the L field but carry on in the same direction at the R of the fields, past a garden hedge and into the golf course (300m). Stay ahead across to the corner of the wood (60m), on beside the trees and down (250m). When the edge of the wood bends R stay ahead across the bottom fairway to the track beside the tall trees (120m). Turn L to the road (50m) and R to the junction in the main part of Harpsden village (50m).*

ⓖ *Walk through the village R to the first field L (120m). Turn L up the path between the fields (100m). Keep on through the trees and up the L edge of the next field then L of a garden (200m).*

ⓗ *Turn R along the road all the way to the end (600m). Turn L to the Peppard Lane (150m).* ➔ⓖ

⑤ Turn R along the road R past the houses L to the wood (200m).

⑥ Turn L along the edge of the wood, R of the drive (80m). Go round a slight bend in the path and down, parallel with the road, into a dip (150m), round a little S-bend and up to the side path R (100m).

⑦ Turn R to the road (50m). Cross and carry on opposite on the woodland path diverging from the road down to the road junction at Harpsden Cemetery (600m).

⑧ Go R along the road past the church (look closely at the sheds opposite) to the L bend (200m). Cut across the bend and follow the pavement over the rise to the 4-way junction in Henley (500m).

⑨ Opposite the tarmac Peppard Lane L turn R down the path which is also Peppard Lane. Keep on to the main road (350m) and cross slightly R (20m) to Mill Lane. Go on to the car park (400m).

Locks are made necessary by weirs. The weirs are needed to raise water levels for navigation but may have originated to drive watermills. The old flash locks were weirs with gateways to allow vessels to be hauled through. The Thames is a highway immemorial. An Act of James I set up a commission to improve the river near Oxford. This led to the building of the first Thames pound locks in 1624. The commission of 1751 was for the whole river above London Bridge. It build 8 pound locks in the 1770s, and others later. Today a lock keeper's prime task is regulating water levels with the weir sluices.

The **tow path** was also the creation of the Thames Commissioners. The river banks were mostly on private land and owners could charge tolls, monopolise the towing or refuse entry. Land for the towpath was bought and owners compensated. Where a landowner refused to sell or to pass gardens, the towpath might be built over the water.

The modern weirs have fish ladders to enable salmon to return to the Upper Thames. Formerly weirs often had fish traps. Fisheries elsewhere, *bucks*, had rows of posts to hold nets; they survived into the age of photography.

The Thames Highway I & II Fred Thacker 1920 & 1968 David & Charles 295+525pp

29 Shiplake, the Thames and Shiplake Woods

About 8¾ km/5½ miles with an extension of 2¼ km/1½ miles to Binsfield Heath and Upper Bolney; river meadows and undulating farmland with bluebell woods
OS maps 1:25000 159 Reading +171 Chiltern Hills W, 1:50000 175 Reading.

Start from a parking spot beside New Road in Lower Shiplake, SU 776 793.
In Upper Shiplake there is a car park at the church hall, SU 767 782.

Linking walks 28❀ 30☆

Baskerville Arms 0118 940 3332
Plowden Arms 0118 940 2794
Orwells 0118 940 3673

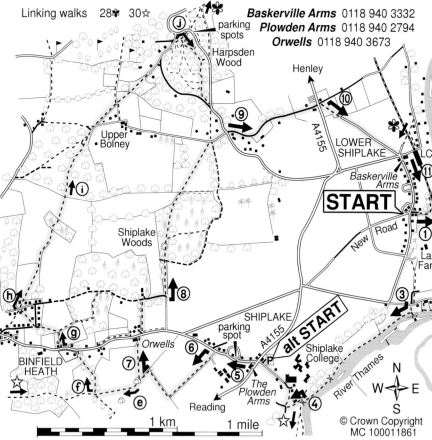

© Crown Copyright
MC 100011861

① Opposite the end of New Road, go along the drive over Lashbrook Stream into the field (130m). Bear L to the corner (50m). Continue out along the path (60m) then R under the railway to the meadow. Aim out of the corner to the footbridge R of the fence halfway across and keep on to the River Thames (400m).

② Outside the field turn R. Follow the bank round a bend, opposite Wargrave, to the railway bridge (1300m). Don't turn R at the bridge but stay beside the river through the gardens (opposite a mouth of the Loddon) (250m). At the shed turn R past the house (70m).

③ Turn L on the road (100m) and take the path after the garden wall back to the river bank (50m). Cross to see the lock (20m) then return. Carry on along the river to the end

58

of the meadow (600m) then below Shiplake College, over the first humped footbridge (150m) to the college boatyard (250m). ☆

④ At the 2nd humped bridge turn R on the level track L of the long shed (120m). Don't join the track at the end but turn R up the steep chalky path to the church (150m). Go L on the lane to the A4155 near the church hall and opposite the **Plowden Arms** (250m).

⑤ Cross the main road and go up Plough Lane. Watch out for the farm drive L (350m).

⑥ Go L along the drive and on at the L edge of the field (450m). Cross the end fence. Follow it R (250m) and round the corner L to the first clump of bushes (80m).

ⓔ *Extension of 2¼ km/1½ miles to Upper Bolney: Stay ahead. A third of the way to the next clump (60m) the path bends ½R across the field (250m).*

ⓕ *In the trees turn R up between fields. Keep on to the road at the pond and well (350m). Walk up the road L to the garden wall R (80m).*

ⓖ *Turn R into the field and follow the L edge (120m). In the next field turn L but diverge from the hedge to the L of the houses (at the edge of Binfield Heath village) (120m). Go on along the drive (40m), over a track and immediately ½R on the path between gardens (150m)*

ⓗ *Over the lane, bear R on the next oblique path between houses to the field. Stay ahead, converging on the R hedge. Go out through*

the corner (350m) and on down the R hedge (200m). At the bottom of the hedge cross ½L to the wood (60m). Go up through the trees (100m) and straight on over the field to the next wood (150m).

ⓘ *Stay ahead through the wood (450m), along the drive to the R bend (50m), into the L field and along the R edge (200m) past side paths at Upper Bolney, between more fields (350m), into the trees and along the tarmac lane to the gravel drive converging L (300m).*

ⓙ *Bear R on the wide side path in the trees (50m) ✿ and turn R on the wide crosspath, which winds near the road and eventually converges on it (500m). Carry on (R) along the road to the junction at the houses (200m). Turn L. ➔⑨*

⑦ At the clump turn back R across the adjacent field to the projecting hedge corner. Stay ahead to the road near **Orwells** (300m), into the field opposite and along the L edge (250m). At the end turn R on the track at Kiln House (200m).

⑧ At the R bend turn L on the path between fields (250m). Stay ahead through the wood to the next field (450m). Cross to the far R corner (400m). ✿ Join the lane and turn R (120m). Carry on across the road.

⑨ Go down the unmade road to the A4155 (700m).

⑩ Cross to the lodge opposite then bear R on the path between the fields (200m). Carry on along the residential street to the junction at the **Baskerville Arms** in the centre of (Lower) Shiplake (500m).

⑪ Cross the road from the railway station and walk along Mill Road to New Road R (400m).

fb
②
brook
WARGRAVE

59

30 Sonning Eye and Shiplake

About 10 km/6¼ miles, undulating farmland and the Thames Path; a short cut of 800m/½mile; extensions of 1 km/¾ mile to Dunsden Green and 4¼ km/2¾ miles to St Patrick's Stream. OS 1:25000 159 Reading, 1:50000 175 Reading.

Start at Sonning Eye; park near the closed end of the lane, SU 749 761.

The Flowing Spring ☎ 0118 969 9878   ***Orwells*** ☎ 0118 940 3673
The Plowden Arms ☎ 0118 940 2794   ***The Bull Inn*** ☎ 0188 969 3901

Linking walk 29☆

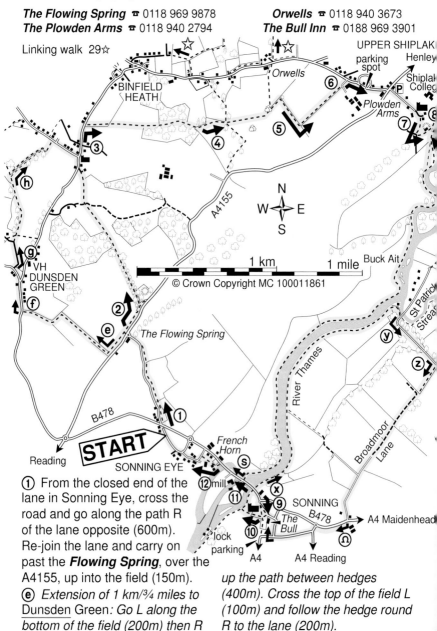

© Crown Copyright MC 100011861

① From the closed end of the lane in Sonning Eye, cross the road and go along the path R of the lane opposite (600m). Re-join the lane and carry on past the ***Flowing Spring***, over the A4155, up into the field (150m).

ⓔ *Extension of 1 km/¾ miles to* Dunsden *Green: Go L along the bottom of the field (200m) then R*

up the path between hedges (400m). Cross the top of the field L (100m) and follow the hedge round R to the lane (200m).

(f) *Walk up the lane R past houses to Dunsden Green (250m). Bear L on the side road (100m).*

(g) *At the end of the green turn R on the track and go round the bend L (200m). When the track bends to the farm, stay ahead to the tree-lined end of the field (450m).*

(h) *Turn R up the edge. The RoW is outside the field but the unofficial path inside is more used. Carry on along the belt of trees and round the bend at the end (350m) then L across to the lane (50m). Turn R to the T-junction (200m), then L. ✦(3)*

(2) Go R up the edge (150m). Near the top proceed outside the field (40m) then turn L. Carry on outside the same field, between woods & over a track (800m) to the road (250m). Go R to the junction (80m).

(3) Stay on the road (200m) then take the path R along the edge of the field, down through the wood and on at the edge (800m).

(4) In the large field, just before the end of the wood, bear L up the slope across the corner then follow the L edge until it bends slightly R (200m). ☆ Cross the path under the trees to the adjacent field L and stay on the same line, diverging ½L from the R edge (250m). Bear L along the far edge past a side path ½L (to **Orwells**) (80m). ☆

(5) Go on to the corner (60m) and R along the fence (250m) then take the path L straight over the field and join the road via the farm drive at Upper Shiplake (450m).

(6) Follow the pavement R, down to the **Plowden Arms** (300m). Cross the A4155 and continue along Church Lane (300m).

(7) Opposite the main gate of the churchyard turn R down the steep path (150m). At the bottom don't continue on the track but turn L through the Shiplake College boat-yard to the River Thames (100m).

(8) Turn R over the humped foot-bridge. Stay ahead on the Thames Path eventually over the long foot-bridge to Sonning Bridge (3500m).

For ✦(x) or ✦(9) turn L on the pavement (80m). For (s), short cut of 800m/½ mile, turn R (200m). ✦(12)

(x) *Extension of 4¼ km/2¾ miles to St Patrick's Stream: At the end of the bridge drop to the path below. Follow the river bank L away from Sonning. Eventually the path bends R at St Patrick's Stream (1900m).*

(y) *Go R on the lane, bending L, to the end of the 1st field R (450m).*

(z) *Take the footpath R along the L edge (250m). Continue on the track (450m) then tarmac past a drive R, and over a rise to the road (500m).*

(n) *On the pavement go R to the junction (250m), L & R on Pearson Road (350m), R down High Street (100m) and L to the pub (50m). ✦(10)*

(9) *Keep on up into Sonning to the L bend (100m). Turn R up into the churchyard (20m) and bear L up the edge to the pub (100m).*

(10) *From the **Bull** cross the churchyard, L of the church. Stay ahead down to the Thames (250m). Turn R and join the road (100m).*

(11) Cross Sonning Bridge (300m).

(12) Opposite the **French Horn** take the footpath near the river round the car park and on between garden walls (200m). At the lane go L and round the R bend to the next lane (200m). Keep on to the parking spot (250m).

31 Ruscombe, the Loddon and Twyford

About 7 km/4½ miles with a 400m extension: a flat walk; farmland and gravel pit country and into Twyford; can be flooded in wet seasons.
OS maps 1:25000 159 Reading 1:50000 175 Reading

Start from Ruscombe Church, SU 797 762.   Linking walks   32✦   33✧

The Waggon & Horses ☎ 0118 934 0376   **The Lands End** ☎ 0118 934 0700
The Duke of Wellington ☎ 0118 934 0456
The Elephant & Castle ☎ 0118 934 0833
The Royal Oak ☎ 0118 934 5190

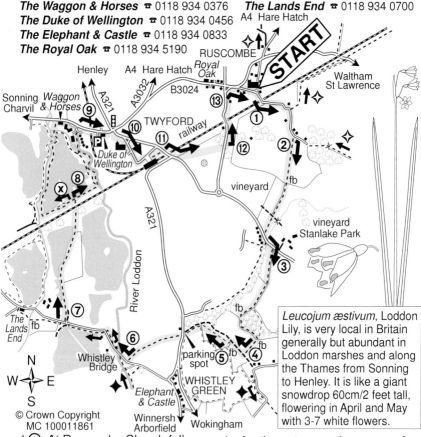

Leucojum æstivum, Loddon Lily, is very local in Britain generally but abundant in Loddon marshes and along the Thames from Sonning to Henley. It is like a giant snowdrop 60cm/2 feet tall, flowering in April and May with 3-7 white flowers.

© Crown Copyright
MC 100011861

✧① At Ruscombe Church follow the lane away from the main road, over the railway. From the bridge carry on along the lane, round the R bend after the house (250m) and round a L bend (150m).

② Turn R into the field, opposite the 2nd of the adjacent houses, and cross slightly L (300m). Over the ditch in the next field, follow the path between fences (250m). Cross the track from Stanlake Park then

aim for the gate near the corner of the field (150m) and join the road.

③ Go L over the brook (30m). After the bridge (60m) take the path R along the L edge to the end of the second field (500m). In the trees turn L over the footbridge. Carry on at the edge of the wood to the next footbridge (150m).

④ Cross it and the field ahead (150m). ✦ On the track outside go R to the next footbridge L (150m).

⑤ Cross into the field L. Turn R and follow the edge of the fields round to the parking area and A321 (400m). Cross and carry on along the path ahead to the lane (400m).

⑥ Walk along the lane R over the River Loddon on Whistley Bridge (80m). Soon after the bridge (70m) join the path R of the lane and carry on to the end (100m). Cross the lane and follow the path on the other side (250m).

⑦ Just after re-joining the lane and after the private side tracks (20m) take the footpath R and keep on under the railway to the path junction at the gravel pit lake (Loddon Nature Reserve) (850m).

ⓧ *Little extension of 400m/¼ mile past the* **Waggon & Horses**: *Go L (250m) and round the corner of the lake. Keep on to the other end and over the cart bridge into the pub car park (700m) then R on the road to the ex-Silk Mill (100m).* ➔⑨

⑧ Go R to the corner of the lake (200m). Turn L either on the public footpath beside the river or on the nature reserve path in the trees. A 20m cross path links them (300m). Just after the link path (20m) cross the river via the mill weir. Continue past the (re-developed) Silk Mill (100m) and cross the millstream to the main road (50m). Turn R

⑨ Go along Twyford High Street, over the railway (Henley line) and past the **Duke of Wellington** to the central crossroads (250m).

⑩ Turn R (80m) then bear R up Station Road past the church (200m). At the top turn L (70m). From the station square go through the arch and up the path beside the railway (100m).

⑪ Cross the main road and the railway (70m). After the bridge (30m) turn L into the recreation ground. Walk away from the main road diverging from the railway to the large gate at the far end (300m).

⑫ Go L along the road, over the railway, to the crossroads in Ruscombe (350m).

The **Royal Oak** is 100m L.

⑬ Turn R along the major road (100m) and fork R on the lane to the church (100m).

Railway Lines in this Book: The line through Ruscombe and Twyford was the Great Western Railway from Paddington to Bristol. Train services started to Maidenhead in 1838 when the station was still in Taplow. After Brunel's brick bridge was built trains ran to Twyford (1839) then Reading (1840). The Bristol section was joined in June 1841 when part of an onward line to Exeter was already operating. The Windsor branch line from Slough was delayed until 1849 because of Eton College opposition. Brunel's Windsor bridge is the oldest wrought iron bridge in use. The brick arches over the floodplain replaced a timber viaduct. Henley is on the end of a line from Twyford (1857) which crosses the Thames at Wargarve. The bridge over to Bourne End from Cock Marsh, was originally timber; it carried the High Wycombe line from Maidenhead (1854) but now terminates at Bourne End. Marlow is on the end of a spur line from Bourne End (1873).

West of London, the London & South West Railway was in competition with the GWR. Its services ran from 1838 and it shifted its London terminus to Waterloo in 1848. The station below Windsor Castle is on the end of the L&SWR branch from Staines (1848). From that sprang the line (1856) to Ascot, Wokingham and Reading.

32 Hurst, Dinton Pastures and the Loddon

About 7½ km/4¾ miles with an extension of 1½ km/1 mile or ¾ km/½ mile more through Dinton Pastures; flat with one gentle rise; farmland, Country Park and river bank. OS maps 1:25000 159 Reading, 1:50000 175 Reading.

Start from the parking area, SU 792 747, beside the A321 near Whistley Green or from Sandford Lane car park (pay) SU 786 727, opposite the Activities Centre drive.

Linking walk 31✦

Green Man ☎ 0118 934 2599
Castle Inn ☎ 0118 934 0034
Jolly Farmer ☎ 0118 934 1881
Elephant & Castle ☎ 0118 934 0886

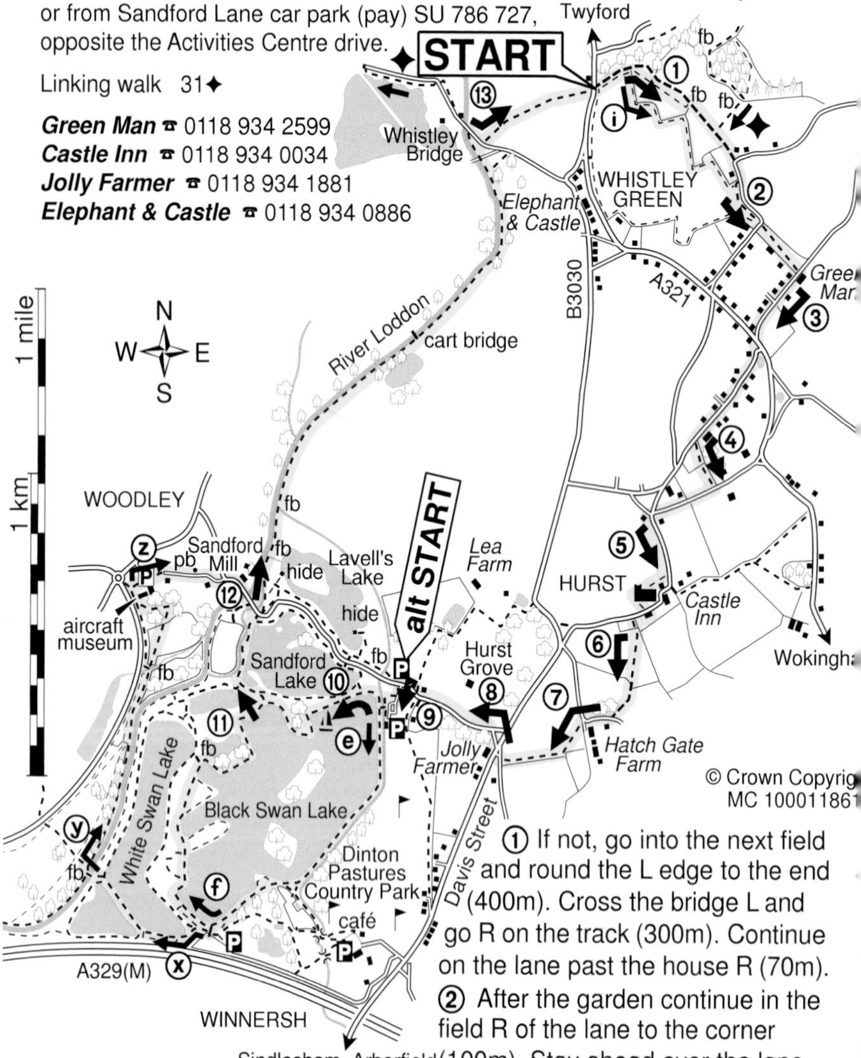

Twyford
✦**START**
WHISTLEY GREEN
Whistley Bridge
Elephant & Castle
River Loddon cart bridge
B3030 A321
Green Mar
WOODLEY
fb
Sandford Mill
pb
Lavell's Lake
hide
hide
aircraft museum
Sandford Lake
alt START
Lea Farm
HURST
Castle Inn
Wokingha
Hurst Grove
Jolly Farmer
Hatch Gate Farm
Black Swan Lake
White Swan Lake
Dinton Pastures Country Park
café
A329(M)
WINNERSH
Sindlesham Arborfield
Davis Street

© Crown Copyrig
MC 100011861

① If not, go into the next field and round the L edge to the end (400m). Cross the bridge L and go R on the track (300m). Continue on the lane past the house R (70m).

② After the garden continue in the field R of the lane to the corner (100m). Stay ahead over the lane, through the narrow field to the next lane at the **Green Man** (200m).

③ Walk along the lane R to the A321 (300m). Cross obliquely L (50m) and go past the pond along School Road (400m).

From the A321 parking area near Whistley Green, enter the large field and go L to the corner (120m). ⓘ If the unofficial path in the field permits, turn R and zigzag round the edge to the house (700m). ✦②

64

④ Turn L into the field after the school. Follow the L edges to the next lane (200m) and turn R on that to the road junction (250m).

⑤ Turn L up Church Hill (250m). Before the bend turn R into Hurst churchyard. Go round the church and over the road to the alms-houses (200m). (**Castle Inn**, L.)

⑥ Go R beside the road (50m), L into the next field and along the L edge (50m) then aim ½R down the field, towards the farmhouse, and follow the track to the lane (300m).

⑦ Go R on the lane to the bend at the farm drive (100m) and into the field opposite. Cut across the L corner then follow the edge to the next lane (400m).

⑧ Turn R to the B3030 at the **Jolly Farmer** (50m). Walk along the lane opposite (50m) then L on Sandford Lane to the car park after the S-bend (300m).

⑨ Opposite the car park, step into the Activities Centre drive (40m) and turn R across the parking area to the stream. Cross the footbridge to Black Swan Lake (100m).

ⓔ *Extension of 1½ km/1 mile: Turn L. Keep to the hard path near the lake past the triangular area at the first major side path (700m), to the 2nd major side path L (from Dinton Pastures overflow car park) (400m). ◆ⓕ or ◆ⓧ*

ⓧ *An extra ¾ km/½ mile past the Woodley aircraft museum: Turn L & R onto the diverging wide path (10m). Keep to the main path round the S-bend and L of White Swan Lake to the R bend in sight of the river footbridge L (500m).*

ⓨ *Cross the River Loddon (50m) and go R beside it (or along the meadow) (750m). When the path splits after a stream, stay ahead over the marsh and up through trees then L to the road (350m). Walk up R beside the road (50m).*

ⓩ *Turn R on the side path past the car park. Cross the museum access drive to the lane (100m). Carry on to the road at Sandford Mill (250m) and R over millstream and river (150m). Turn L. ◆⑫*

ⓕ *Stay on the same broad path past the path from the footbridge L (700m) and on at the water's edge round lots of bends to the next major path junction (600m). ◆⑪*

⑩ Go R on the wide path round the corner of the lake, passing a side path R (100m). Stay beside the lake (200m), L & R round a headland and on to the next major path junction (300m).

⑪ Turn away from the lake on the curving side path (150m). Pass a side path L and go round the R curve. Carry on beside the River Loddon and cross the road (300m).

⑫ Carry on along the Loddon all the way to the end of the path at Whistley road Bridge (1800m). ◆

⑬ Turn R on the road (50m) and L on the path to the A321 opposite the parking place (450m).

Whistley was the ancient manor on which Twyford, Hurst and Sindlesham arose. It is Uuiscelea in the Abingdon Abbey Chronicles, recording its grant in 986 by king Edgar of Wessex to his thegn Wulfstan who had given it to the abbey. It is WISELEI in the Domesday Book, with land for 12 ploughs and woods taxed at 50 pigs. The Normans incorporated it into Windsor Forest, where it became part of Bear Wood walk. The medieval manor house was at Whistley Court Farm. Until 1844 it was a detached part of Wiltshire.

33 Ruscombe and West End Farm

About 7 km/4½ miles; level through wheat fields; good for train spotters.
An extension of 4¼ km/2¾ miles to Hare Hatch may may be used as a separate short walk. OS maps 1:25000 159 Reading, 1:50000 175 Reading.

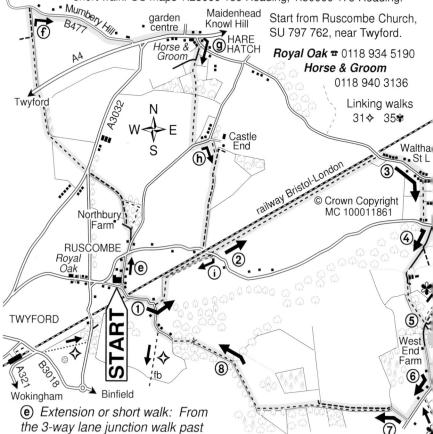

Start from Ruscombe Church, SU 797 762, near Twyford.

Royal Oak ☎ 0118 934 5190
Horse & Groom
0118 940 3136

Linking walks
31◇ 35❋

© Crown Copyright
MC 100011861

(e) *Extension or short walk: From the 3-way lane junction walk past Ruscombe Church along the lane with most houses (250m). Cross the main road and follow Castle End Road (100m). After the house bear L on the track which soon curves L (150m). At the farm gates turn R on the lesser track and stay on it to the A3032 (450m). Cross into the field opposite. Go straight up through the top corner (350m), R along the edge of the next field and on to the A4 (350m). Cross and stay ahead up the fields to the next road, the B477 (600m).*

(f) *Turn R and go down the lane to the A4 (800m). Walk along the pavement L (450m).*

(g) *Cross to the **Horse & Groom** and follow the Waltham side road briefly (50m). After the houses turn R on the farm drive. At the R bend stay ahead on the path through the small wood and across the next field to the L corner (650m).*

(h) *Go L along the road to the L bend (150m). Just into the Business Park drive R, take the path R along the edge of the field*

66

(100m). Bear R on the track and stay on it down to the road (600m). Pass under the railway to the side paths L & R (50m). If continuing on the main route turn L. ➔②

ⓘ *If cutting back to Ruscombe, turn R up the steps in the thicket. Follow the railway fence (350m) then descend L to the field and follow the R edge. Near the corner bear R to the lane (250m). Follow the lane R to the church (350m).*

① At Ruscombe Church take the lane over the railway (300m). On the R bend, just after the house L, take the path L and bear L along the end of the field to the railway (250m).The public footpath is up the steps through the hedge and along the railway fence but there is sometimes an unofficial path along the hedge. Continue to the next road, at the bridge (350m).

② Stay beside the railway to the next road, at houses (1400m). ✽

③ Walk along the road R (350m). On the L curve, watch out for the footpath R between gardens. Follow it to the next road (300m).

④ Go L along the road (70m) and turn R along the farm track (150m). After the bridge bear R on the main track over another stream (250m). When the track bends to stables stay ahead near the L edge and into the next field. The path soon diverges from the R edge to the gate on the far side (350m).

⑤ Outside, turn R on the track and continue on tarmac past West End Farm to the road (450m).

⑥ Walk along the road R (300m).

⑦ Opposite Blackthorn Farm turn R on the hard farm track (150m). At the next field bear L. The public

bridleway is between the fields but people also use the track at the edge (500m). Continue at the edge in the next field (500m), round the corner R and on to the tree-lined end of the field (350m).

⑧ Bear L along the edge of the next field (300m). Stay ahead over the ditch and through trees (150m) to a house ◈ and carry on along the winding lane to the railway bridge (550m) and Ruscombe.

The **Great Western Railway** opened to Twyford in 1839. In the previous decade there were several successful short and/or private steam railways that led to the notion of trunk railways with numerous stations and uses. The GWR was the fifth trunk railway, preceded only by the the the Baltimore & Ohio Rail Road of 1830, the South Carolina Rail Road of 1831, the Grand Junction Railway of 1837 (N from Birmingham) and the London & SW Railway whose first train ran to Woking in 1838, only a week before the first GWR train to Maidenhead.

A Bristol railway had been proposed in 1824 but the GWR was not set up until 1833. It appointed Brunel, aged 27, as Engineer. His rail design and engine specifications caused serious teething problems but he became the great driver of the project. The branch lines to Gloucester and Oxford were in the original plan but the GWR went on expanding to Cornwall, Wales and the Midlands, often absorbing local railways. The GWR was compelled to convert from its broad gauge of 7ft to the 4' 8½" of other railways in 1892.

Daniel Gooch, aged 20, became the superintendent of locomotive engines in 1837. He built engines from 1846 at the new Swindon works and became GWR chairman. He commissioned the Atlantic telegraph cable (1865). He was made baronet. He lies in the SW corner of Clewer churchyard.

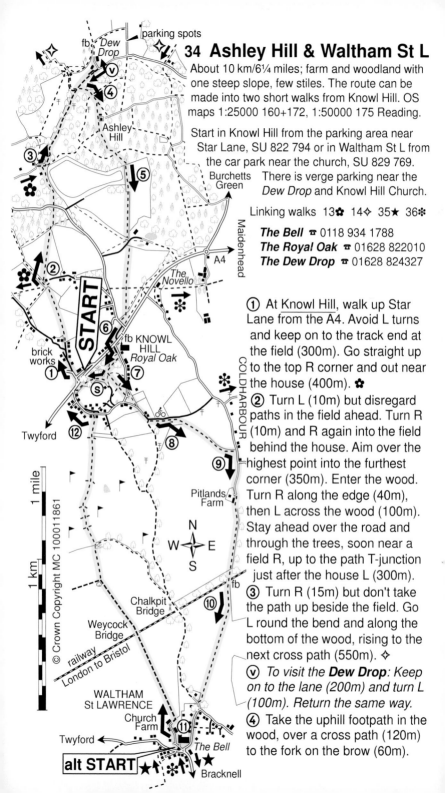

parking spots

fb *Dew Drop*

34 Ashley Hill & Waltham St L

About 10 km/6¼ miles; farm and woodland with one steep slope, few stiles. The route can be made into two short walks from Knowl Hill. OS maps 1:25000 160+172, 1:50000 175 Reading.

Start in Knowl Hill from the parking area near Star Lane, SU 822 794 or in Waltham St L from the car park near the church, SU 829 769. There is verge parking near the *Dew Drop* and Knowl Hill Church.

Ⓥ

④

Ashley Hill

⑤

Burchetts Green

Linking walks 13✿ 14✧ 35★ 36❋

The Bell ☎ 0118 934 1788
The Royal Oak ☎ 01628 822010
The Dew Drop ☎ 01628 824327

③

②

A4

The Novello

❋

START

⑥ fb KNOWL HILL *Royal Oak*

brick works

①

Ⓢ

⑦

Twyford

⑫

⑧

⑨

Pitlands Farm

① At Knowl Hill, walk up Star Lane from the A4. Avoid L turns and keep on to the track end at the field (300m). Go straight up to the top R corner and out near the house (400m). ✿

② Turn L (10m) but disregard paths in the field ahead. Turn R (10m) and R again into the field behind the house. Aim over the highest point into the furthest corner (350m). Enter the wood. Turn R along the edge (40m), then L across the wood (100m). Stay ahead over the road and through the trees, soon near a field R, up to the path T-junction just after the house L (300m).

③ Turn R (15m) but don't take the path up beside the field. Go L round the bend and along the bottom of the wood, rising to the next cross path (550m). ✧

Ⓥ *To visit the **Dew Drop**: Keep on to the lane (200m) and turn L (100m). Return the same way.*

④ Take the uphill footpath in the wood, over a cross path (120m) to the fork on the brow (60m).

⑩

fb

Chalkpit Bridge

Weycock Bridge

railway

London to Bristol

COLDHARBOUR

© Crown Copyright MC 100011861

1 mile

1 km

N W E S

WALTHAM St LAWRENCE

Church Farm

⑪

Twyford ←

The Bell

alt START ★ ✿ ❋ ★

Bracknell

Fork R past the house on Ashley Hill (100m). Stay ahead down through trees to the field (400m).

⑤ Go down the R hedge to the bend (200m), then on the other side of the hedge. Stay ahead to the farm drive (300m). Cross into field beyond ❀ and aim diagonally for the bottom corner (500m).

⑥ Exit L of the corner and turn R. Converge on the main road. Over the side road follow the track then cross at the footbridge or a traffic island (150m). Go up the side road at the church (80m). Halfway to the *Royal Oak*, diverge R up into the trees of the Common. Follow the path up to the grassy top (150m).

⑤ *Short cut halving the route: Carry on along the top of the hill skirting R of the gardens into the wood and down to the main road almost opposite Star Lane (300m).*

⑦ Go down the hill converging on the road L (200m). Over the road follow the L hedge into the corner of the Common (100m) and turn L along the lane (120m). ❀

⑧ After the end house, disregard a path R but transfer to the path R of the cycle track (200m). After the electricity substation bear R over

the field. Continue along the L hedge to the next road (500m).

⑨ Go R on the road (80m). When it bends L, stay ahead on the drive (200m). At the house continue ahead past the end of the garden and along the L hedge to the London-Bristol railway (600m).

⑩ Cross the bridge and continue along the L hedge (150m). Before it bends L, bear R over the field. Aim for the cluster of houses and the church then next to the garden hedge (700m). From the gate go L to the road at the bend (40m) and R along the road to the *Bell* in Waltham St Lawrence (250m). ★

⑪ Cross the frontage of the churchyard and walk along the drive of Church Farm towards the farm house then R at the garden past the farm buildings (200m). At the end of the farmyard turn R & L to the field then stay ahead: over the railway (650m) past the L bend in the track (450m) to the end of the field (200m) and between golf course hedges to the road at Knowl Hill village (800m).

⑫ Follow the road L, round the knoll, to the A4 (250m). Turn R and cross to Star Lane (50m).

North Star used to pass under the bridges of this walk. It pulled the first scheduled train of the Great Western Railway from Taplow to Paddington on 4th June 1838. Intended for the New Orleans Railway, it had to be modified for the wide gauge of the GWR and was their most powerful and reliable early locomotive. It was built at Newcastle-on-Tyne by Robert Stephenson and delivered by sea to London then barge to Maidenhead.

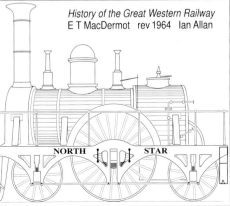

History of the Great Western Railway
E T MacDermot   rev 1964   Ian Allan

NORTH   STAR

35 Waltham St L, Shottesbrooke and West End

About 8 km/5 miles with a short cut of 1 km/¾ mile. Gently undulating fields and stretches of lane. OS maps: 1:25000 159 or 160, 1:50000 175 Reading.

Start at the village hall car park near Waltham St Lawrence church, SU 829 769, or from the Downfield Road kerb, 1 km/¾ miles S of the village, SU 832 758.

The Bell ☎ 0118 934 1788   Linking walks   33❀   34★   36✳   37✦
The Star ☎ 0118 934 3486
The Royal Oak ☎ 0118 934 5133

© Crown Copyright
MC 100011861

★✳① From the church in Waltham St Lawrence, walk along the street past the **Bell** and a field R (300m). Opposite the timber-framed Paradise Cottage turn L along the wall to the end of the 1st field (200m). Cross the L corner of the next field and the corner of the little wood (100m) and carry on in the same line over the next field to the L corner near a pair of houses (250m). Cross the lane and go straight on beside the garden and into the trees (400m). After the wood enter the field R but keep on in the same direction beside the haha of Shottesbrooke Park (150m) then under trees and through the garden tunnel to Shottesbrooke Church (150m). ✦

② After the church turn R. Don't stay on the drive but keep near the park boundary to the corner and under the trees to the road (350m). Cross 20m R and go along the track, past the house, and round the curve into the field (150m). Aim for the top corner (200m). Stay ahead on the path between fields to the next road (1100m). Turn R to the road junction (20m) then L.

③ Follow the wider road over the bridge (100m). After the second house R take the diverging path R of the garden. Go on between fields to the next road (700m).

④ Turn R to the road junction in West End (150m) and L away from School Road (100m).

Ⓢ *Short cut of 1 km/¾ mile: Stay on the lane to the end (450m) then bear L along the road (150m).* ✦⑧

⑤ At the bend turn L on the track to Goosenest Cottage (150m). Pass R of the house down the path between fields (100m). After the ditch, go straight over the field L of isolated trees to the road (300m).

⑥ Walk along the road R (70m) and take the footpath R along the edge of the wood (250m). After the large ditch cross the field ahead to the corner of the next wood (200m).

⑦ Just into the trees turn L & R and follow the garden fence along the edge of the wood (100m). At the fields stay at the R edge to the road (250m). ✿ Turn R (100m).

⑧ On the bend turn off along Mire Lane past West End Farm (250m). After the tarmac, keep on around the curve to the drive R (150m).

⑨ Enter the field L. Don't go straight over but follow the R edge. In the next field make for the far R corner and rejoin the track (350m). Carry on (L) to the road (200m).

⑩ Cross into the field. Make for the R end, converging on the trees (250m). In the next field cross obliquely L to the corner (150m). Follow the garden boundary into the next field (60m), R round the bend and along the edge (150m).

⑪ Halfway along stay on the path when it bends L across the field (150m). At the houses turn R and walk along the road towards the church (150m).

The **Bell** is of interest as a building and a charity. The middle part was a narrow smoke hall of about 1400. The flanking rooms with the jettied upper storey would have been added soon after but the upper floor in the middle was not inserted over the hall until about 1600. Ralph Newberry bought the house in 1596. At his death in 1607 it was left to eleven villagers as trustees to lease for alms; a framed copy of the indenture is on display in the pub. By 1723 the tenant was a victualler at the sign of the bell. The pub is now a charitable trust. Ralph Newberry was born in the parish. He was a printer and publisher, who set up his presses 84 years after Caxton. Master of the Printing House to Elizabeth I and James I, he brought to the world Camden's *Britannia,* in 1586. He is in the list of benefactors on the south wall of the church nave.

Waltham St Lawrence lies on the route of the Camlet Way, the Roman road from St Albans to Silchester. The name (*weald ham*, forest enclosure) first appears in 940 in a grant of land to Alfsige by King Edmund. This must have been subdivided soon after for there were three manors of WALTHÃ in the Domesday Book. It was crown land at that time but in medieval times went to the bishops of Winchester. The church is a hotchpotch of styles. The chancel was re- built in the 13th century and the nave extended to join it. Points of interest: round unadorned Norman arches at the west end, the Norman south door within the porch; a fragment of ancient fresco on the east pillar of the north aisle; the relief memorial in the north chapel of Sir Henry Neville who bought the manor after Dissolution of the Monasteries.

36 Waltham St L, Knowl Hill and Shottesbrooke

About 8½ km/5¼ miles with an extension of 1¼ km/¾ mile via Littlewick Green; farmland, gentle slopes, few stiles, slippery in winter. OS maps 1:25000 159 Reading +172 Chiltern Hills East or 160 Windsor +172, 1:50000 175 Reading.

Start at Waltham St Lawrence, parking at the village hall, SU 829 769, or, on the extension, at Knowl Hill, parking in the side road at the church, SU 824 795.

The Royal Oak ☎ 01628 822010   **The Cricketers** ☎ 01628 822888
The Bell ☎ 0118 934 1788   **The Novello** ☎ 01628 825753

Linking walks
34✤   35✱   37☆

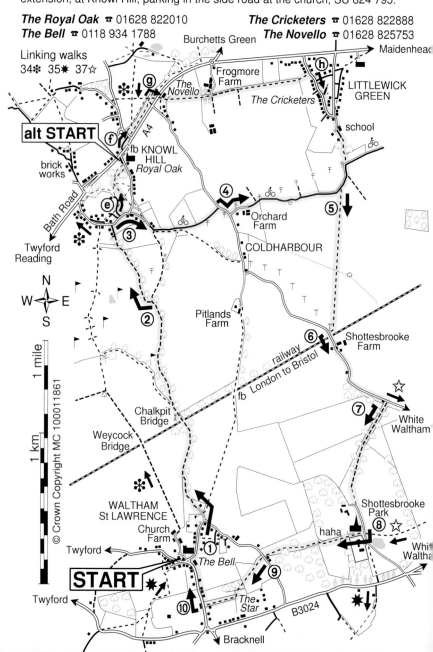

✻① At Waltham St Lawrence go along Halls Lane between the churchyard and the **Bell** (300m). At the R bend bear L along the drive then track (700m). After the (London-Bristol) railway bridge (100m) disregard a side path L and carry on beside the golf course to the next track junction (750m).

② Take the side track L, soon curving R. Keep on to Knowl Hill village (550m). Turn R on the lane.

ⓔ *Extension of 1¼ km/¾ mile: Soon (70m), cut across the 1st drive L and go up the 2nd (100m), R over the grass into the trees on the top and down the path R to the road below the* **Royal Oak** *(250m). Descend L to the A4 (100m).*

ⓕ *Turn R. Cross the A4 a.s.a.p. and stay ahead out of the village, through the parking area, over the side road (150m), then parallel with the A4 through the field and trees or along the edge of the L field to the next gate, watching out for the Shottesbrook side road (300m).*

ⓖ *Soon after the side road (80m) cross the A4 and the grass to the* **Novello** *(50m). Behind the pub take the footpath across the field to the coniferous R corner of the farmstead (250m). Stay ahead along the top edge of the next field then between gardens to the road in Littlewick Green (800m).*

ⓗ *Turn R. Walk along the village green past the* **Cricketers** *to the far corner (350m) and continue on School Lane (100m). Stay ahead on the track into the corner of a large field (250m) and around the curving the R edge. Disregard the side track L (70m) but join the diverging path after it (50m).* ➤⑤

③ Stay on the lane R round to the farmhouse on the bend (100m) and ahead on the side lane (200m). After the end house, disregard the paths R and bear L along the cycle track to the next road (500m).

④ Turn R on the road (100m) and L on the drive round the farm buildings (150m). Continue on the cycle track over the fields (550m) and along a hedge (200m). Just round the L bend join the footpath back R (50m before a side track R).

⑤ Go straight over the field; aim for the house R of the farm, almost in line with the church spire (950m).

⑥ Cross the railway bridge and go on along the road (300m), round the S-bend and on to the next house R, Middle Lodge (350m). ☆

⑦ Turn R along the lime avenue in Shottesbrooke Park (600m) then bear L over the grass towards the manor house and follow the drive past the garden to Shottesbrooke Church (350m). ✳

⑧ Take the side path R past the church, under an arch and trees (100m) then along the R edge of the field (250m). Continue at the L edge of the next field then through more trees to the road (400m).

⑨ Cross the field opposite. Aim slightly L to the trees, mid far side (250m) and cut across the small wood (100m) and the corner of the next field (50m). Bear R on the path between fields to the road in Waltham St Lawrence (200m).

⑩ Turn R for the church (300m).

| Fences near the railway may have lengths of iron from the original GWR line of Brunel distinguished by their top hat cross section. |

37 White Waltham and Shottesbrooke

About 8 km/5 miles through the village, parkland and gently rolling arable farmland. OS maps: 1:25000 160 Windsor, 1:50000 175 Reading.

Start at White Waltham, parking in the side road, Walgrove Gardens, near the *Bee Hive*, SU 849 771. Groups may park at the village hall with permission (☎ 01628 822014). There are parking spots at the north corner of the green.

The Bee Hive ☎ 01628 822877   ***Waltham Place Tea Room*** ☎ 01628 825517

① From Walgrove Gardens in White Waltham cross the road and the cricket green opposite the ***Bee Hive*** to the side path half way round the perimeter fence (150m). Follow the path to Shottesbrooke Park (250m) and go straight over to the church (400m). ♦☆ It is worth collecting the key to see inside.

② From the church follow the drive R past Shottesbrooke Park house (150m). When the drive bends L to the house stay ahead over the grass almost to the fence (200m) then bear R along the lime avenue to the Gothic lodge (600m).

③ Turn R on the road (350m). After the first houses L see White Waltham airfield L. Continue to the row of houses (500m).

④ Turn L outside the field before the houses and follow the fence round L & R bends (100m) to the path with steps R (60m). Cross the the dip and follow the R fence up to the parish hall car park (200m).

⑤ Outside the car park turn L on the pavement (150m). Just after the lane L (40m) cross into the field. Make for the top L corner (150m) and keep on to the road (100m).

⑥ Walk down the pavement L, through the churchyard and on to the main road (300m).

⑦ At the junction, find the footpath behind the trees R and follow the edge of the field (100m) then walk

74

away from the road at the L edge of the field to the lane (350m). Go L (20m) then R on the tarmac farm road over the fields (750m). ✳

⑧ Near the bend L at the farm buildings take the track R across the field and up the L edge (550m).

⑨ At the wood diverge R round the trees into the next field (150m). Turn R along the edge. The path is in the trees initially (150m) then re-enters the field and goes round the corner (300m) and up L towards the motorway (500m).

⑩ At the end of the wood turn R into the next field and follow the R edges to the B3024 (450m).

⑪ Walk along the road R (100m) then the side road R to the ornate gates of Waltham Place (300m).

⑫ Cross to the L edge of the field opposite and follow it away from the road (200m). Continue in the next field towards the house at the bottom R corner (170m) and round the end to exit L of it (30m). Keep on in the same direction through Walgrove Gardens (200m).

One of the two Domesday Book entries for White Waltham - printed actual size

The line through place names was red for highlighting, not deletion. The hand writing is Caroline miniscule used over much of Europe at that time and is still easy to read. The words in Latin were uniformly abbreviated: Tra=*terra*, land; m̊ = *modo*, now. TRE = *tempore regis Edwardi* = in the time of *king* Edward ie prior to the Conquest. The entries were recorded on parchment in 1086, probably at Winchester which was the site of the Exchequer until the 13th century. The folios are 15x11", approx A3, with entries in order of county, owner and hundred in two columns on both sides. The uniform layout and highlighting would have made it easy for a clerk to surf through the folios as a database to assess tax but there is no record of why William the Conqueror made the survey. By 1200 the 413 skins had been made into a book entitled *Liber de Wintonia*, Book of Winchester. The *Domesday* name appears in early court records but was probably satirical in origin; this was the first bureaucratic tool for the whole of England; tax was set until doomsday. The book is on display at the Public Records Office in Kew.

BERKSHIRE

XI LAND OF THE CHURCH OF CHERTSEY   In BEYNHURST Hundred

The Abbey of Chertsey holds WALTHAM for the domestic victualling of the mo nks; TRE it held it. Then & now it answered for x hides. Land for xii ploughs. In demesne are ii ploughs. xviii villeins with x ploughs. There is i serf & a little church; & ix acres of pasture. Woodland at v pigs.   with 2 cottagers
Of this land Thorold holds i hide and a virgate from the abbot; there^he has ii ploughs. Total TRE viii pounds; now the part of the Abbot vi pounds, of Thorold x shillings.

38 Ockwells, Stud Green and Paley Street

About 9¾ km/6 miles with a very short version of 3¾ km/2½ miles; flat farmland; little shade. OS maps 1:25000 160 Windsor, 1:50000 175 Reading.

Start from Cox Green at Ockwells Park car park, SU 878 790, or from Paley Street, parking by the roadside at north end of Sheepcote Lane, SU 870 762.

Linking walks 37✳ 39✳ 42❖

The Bridge House 01628 623288
The Royal Oak 01628 620541

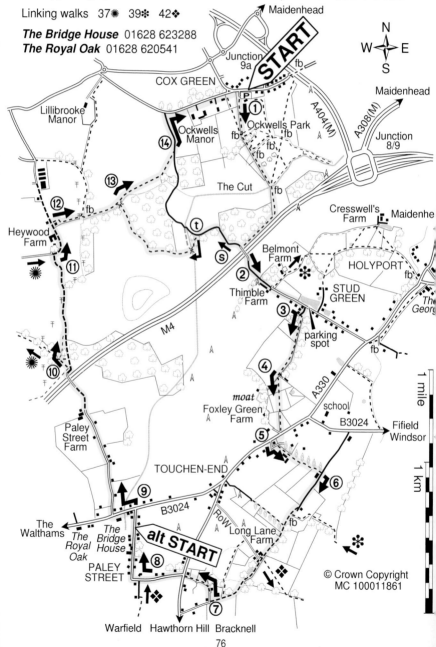

© Crown Copyright
MC 100011861

① At Ockwells Park walk away from the road beside the R hedge. Stay ahead over the footbridges. After the wide stream, the Cut, continue beside the wood (800m). Follow the path R, under trees beside the M4 to the end (350m).

Ⓢ *Short version: Turn R along the byway (250m) which bends L after the wood. On the next R curve watch out for a side path L (200m).*

Ⓣ *Follow the side path over the footbridge (100m), across past the end of the wood (100m) and round beside the trees to the stream (600m). Cross and turn R.* ➔⑬

② Turn L over the M4 and stay on the track past farm drives R & L (350m). ✽ Continue on the tarmac lane through Stud Green (300m).

③ Halfway along the long pond turn R on Rolls Lane (100m). At the end take the footpath L beside the ditch under trees to the fields (100m). Carry on at the L edge near the boundary ditch (300m).

④ Just after the side track over the ditch and 100m before the tree-lined end, turn into the L field. Follow the bisecting line out of the corner and cross the paddocks to the far hedge corner (400m).

⑤ Cross the A330. Walk along the pavement R (100m) then turn L on the farm drive (50m). Go round the L bend (50m) and, at the garden gates, take the horse track R past stables and paddocks to the next vehicle track (400m).

⑥ Walk along the track R (300m). After the house continue on the bridleway past the farmyard at Long Lane Farm (400m), ❖ past a pond R (100m) and ahead up to the tarmac lane (400m).

⑦ Turn R on the drive and continue on the track into the field L (100m). Follow the L edge of the field and continue ahead to the A330 (200m). Cross to Sheepcote Lane and follow it to the R bend in Paley Street (350m).

⑧ Go round the bend and on to the B3024 at the other end (500m).

⑨ Go L on the pavement, over the Cut (150m). Just after the **Bridge House** cross to the lane R. Follow it to the end of the tarmac (800m) and continue on the track over the M4 (300m).

⑩ At the L bend below the motorway, enter the field L and cross the corner (100m). ✳ Pass through the hedge and along the edge of the trees to re-join the track (150m). Keep on to the T-junction (550m).

⑪ Follow the track R, round L to the first house R (250m).

⑫ After the house, turn R on the footpath. Skirt the garden and the edge of the field (250m). At the corner cross the footbridge and keep on along the edge of the next field near the stream and wood, past a footbridge R (300m).

⑬ Keep on along the field. After the wood aim for the distant, big house, Ockwells Manor (500m).

⑭ Turn L along the track (Thrift Lane) (300m) and R along the road to the car park R (500m).

Paley Street's name is not on record until 1711, too recent for etymological explanation. *Pægan leah,* Pæga's clearing, is a possibility for Paley. **Touchen-End** probably derives from Touchen Lane End. *Twychene* is recorded in 1274. Old English: *twicen* a road fork. **Thrift Lane** most likely derives from Frith, wood. *Place-Names of Berkshire* Margaret Gelling CUP 1973 955p

39 Holyport, Mount Skippets and Stud Green

About 8 km/5 miles; almost level farmland on the London Clay; the fields flood in very wet conditions. OS maps 1:25000 160 Windsor, 1:50000 175 Reading.

Start from Holyport village green, SU 892 778; park in a side road near one of the pubs. Large groups should ask to park at the Memorial Hall car park.

Linking walks 38❋ 40✦ 41❋ 42★

The Belgian Arms ☎ 01628 634468   **The Sun & Stars** ☎ 01628 623639
The White Hart ☎ 01628 621460   **The Jolly Gardner** ☎ 01628 622933
The George ☎ 01628 628317

(a) *If starting at the Memorial Hall, turn R from the car park. Opposite the side road R (100m), turn L on the track between houses. Go round the edge of the field to the path under the trees between fields (250m). Turn R (250m).*
(b) *In the next field L take the diagonal path across the middle (200m). Likewise in the next field: cross to the far corner (300m).* ✦(4)

✦(1) At Holyport cross the village green to the end furthest from the main road, A330 (100m) and take the narrow path R of the garden of the timber-framed house to the next road (150m). Turn L (150m).

② On the S-bend turn R along the vehicle track, past the houses and sports ground ✳ to the end of the wood L (400m) and on to the side tracks of Oak Tree Farm R (250m).

③ Enter the field R after the sheds and diverge from the track to the far corner (150m). Cross the ditch to the L field and follow the R hedge to the next road (450m).

④ Cross the road and take the track, R of the **Sun & Stars**, up to Mount Skippets. Pass the farm to the end of the track (1000m) and go down the L edge of the fields to the 2nd footbridge (300m). ★

⑤ Soon after the ditch (70m), at a garden corner L, turn R across the field, converging slightly on the R edge (250m). Continue in the next fields up the track (200m). ✳

⑥ Outside, turn R on the large track, passing a house in the trees R. Continue down the bridleway to the stream (250m).

⑦ Next to the bridge turn L into the field, crossing another stream (40m). Follow the R edge up next to the ditch (500m). At the end of the ditch near the top of the field turn R (70m). Go round the corner L and into the side field R. Follow the L hedge to the garden (250m). Skirt round it and cross the footbridge to the bridleway (100m).

⑧ Turn R past the house and continue on the track to the end of the large shed L (350m).

⑨ Turn L on the horse track past paddocks (400m). At the house drive go L & R to the road (100m).

⑩ Turn R along the pavement (100m) then cross into the corner of the field beside the farm drive. Look across the paddocks for the furthest hedge corner diagonally and aim for it from gate to gate (400m). In the next field follow the ditch R along the fields and ahead under trees to the houses at Stud Green (400m). Turn R to the lane opposite the large pond (100m).

⑪ Turn R to the end of the pond (80m) then L on the shared drive. After the gardens keep on between fields and into a field (250m). Cross to where the trees appear to end at the R edge (150m).

⑫ Go on at the R edge of the fields beside trees (450m) and into the L corner of a large field. Now keep near the L edge to Holyport (200m). Cross the footbridge and pass under trees to the main road and village green (50m). ☆

*Ⓨ For the Memorial Hall, cross to the **George** and go R on the path on the green, parallel with the A330 (500m).*

Ⓩ At the tarmac drive bear L to the gates (50m) then L along the track to the next road (400m). The Hall is 100m L.

The garden weed that looks like a 30cm Christmas tree is common horsetail, *Equisetum arvense* (not marestail). It spreads with a dense mat of thin rhizomes. In Spring they put up short stems with spore cones, often hidden in grass. Like ferns, the spores produce a different unseen plant which reproduces sexually. Whereas ferns are mainly leaf, horsetails are mainly stem. Most of the other British species are taller and have cones on top of their main stems.

x¼

40 Holyport and Bray Lake

About 8¼ km/5 miles, through the village and over almost flat farmland on the London Clay. OS maps 1:25000 160 Windsor, 1:50000 175 Reading.

Start at Holyport, SU 892 778; park beside a road at the edge of the village green. Groups may obtain permission to use the large Memorial Hall car park. Alternatively start at Bray Lake car park, SU 912 786, near Bray Marina.

Linking walks
20❀ 21✿ 22❀ 39✦ 41✳

The Belgian Arms ☎ 01628 634468
The White Hart ☎ 01628 621460
The George ☎ 01628 628317

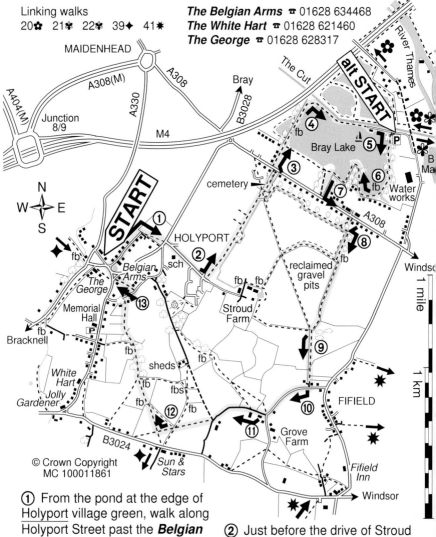

© Crown Copyright
MC 100011861

① From the pond at the edge of Holyport village green, walk along Holyport Street past the **Belgian Arms**. Philberds was at the end of the road (300m). In the field turn R and exit near the corner (200m). Cross the main road and go along Stroud Farm Road (400m).

② Just before the drive of Stroud Farm take the path L (700m). At the end of the fields watch for the entrance to the cemetery slightly R. Go through the middle and L of the chapel. Cross the road (200m).

80

③ Stay ahead at the L edge of the field to Bray Lake and on (600m).

④ Go round the end and on along the track. ✿ (The 1st bridge L leads to more gravel pit lakes and paths.) Go past the sailing club to the next corner of the lake (550m). ❀

⑤ Just after the corner take the path R in the trees around the lake over the creek footbridge (400m).

⑥ Stay near the water round the corner of the lake then out round a headland protruding into the lake (500m). After the headland turn R along the straight shore (120m).

⑦ At the next bulge in the shore line turn L, up the edge of the field, soon beside trees and a garden, to the road (150m). Walk L along the pavement (250m).

⑧ Just after Tithe Barn Drive L (20m) take the footpath R between buildings to the T-junction (100m). Turn L (50m). Pass round a R bend in the trees, up to the fields (200m). After the footbridge go round the corner of the hedge (20m) and up the path L of the hedge to the cross path in the field at the top (500m).

⑨ Turn L and stay ahead to the lane at Fifield (400m). ✳

⑩ Walk along the lane R (400m).

⑪ At Coningsby Farm turn R on Green Lane (with deep ditches) (400m). In the R field immediately after the next side track, cross on the bisecting line to the hedge, 150m before the road (300m). ✦

⑫ In the next field get to the next corner R. The turning place is in the middle (100m) where diagonal rights of way cross but when the field is boggy there is usually an unofficial path along the R edge to the next exit (250m). Go over the footbridge into the next field and cross diagonally to the far corner (150m). Outside follow the path between fields to the end (550m).

⑬ Walk along the road R (100m) then turn L on the footpath (150m) and cross Holyport village green.

Thames valley
Winter Hill Gravels
Taplow Gravels
Flood Plain Gravels

Bray Lake is a flooded **gravel pit** which has been put to use for water sports. Since the 1930s hundreds of such pits have been dug in the flood plains of the Thames and its tributaries to supply the gravel for London concrete. Other pits have become nature reserves, parks and landfill sites. Some are still active for extraction, landfill and reclamation.

The gravel is mostly flint washed out of the chalk of the Chiltern Hills and North Downs during the Ice Age. Bray Lake gravel was the river bed of the last glaciation (Devensian) ending about 10 000 years ago. Alluvium has raised the present river and floodplain upon it.

From Trafalgar Square to Maidenhead, 10m above the river, are the Taplow Gravels. These are early Devensian, 100 000 years old, and get their name from where they were first examined. Dry pits for these gravels were under the fields of this walk above the A308. After filling with refuse they have now been re-landscaped; the iron pipes are for instruments to monitor pollution. Hippopotamus fossils show there was a warm period within this glaciation.

Higher still, little pits eg at Burnham Beeches are the Winter Hill Gravels representing the river bed during the Anglian Glaciation of ½m years ago.

41 Fifield, Braywood and New Lodge

About 9¾ km/6 miles with an extension of 500m and a short cut of 3¾ km/2¼ miles; gently undulating farm country on the London Clay. Lots of stiles.
OS maps 1:25000 160 Windsor, 1:50000 175 Reading.

Start from the layby on Drift Road near Fifield Lane, SU 908 752.

Linking walks 39✳ 40✳   *The Fifield Inn* ☎ 01628 626512

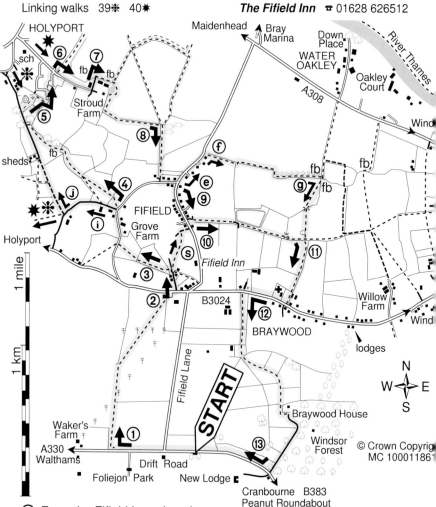

① From the Fifield Lane junction walk along Drift Road (W) past the gates of Foliejon Park (250m). After the drive (150m) watch out for the gap to the field R and take the path down the L edge (Foliejon soon visible behind) (550m). At the start of the hedge bear R over the field, aiming just L of the barn near the bottom R corner at Fifield (650m).

② A little way along the road R (50m) turn L on Ledger Lane to the three footpaths at the end (150m).

Ⓢ *Short cut of 3¾ km/2¼ miles: Stay ahead on the path diverging R*

82

from the end drive (250m). Turn R on the track (50m) and L on the road (50m). →⑩

③ Take the L footpath to the next lane (400m). Walk along the lane R round past Grove Farm to the broad track L after Coningsby Farm (Green Lane) (300m). ❋✳

ⓘ *If the fields are flooded in wet winters, follow Green Lane (400m).*

ⓙ *Go R on the first side track (Gay's Lane) to the end of the little wood R after the fields (750m).* →⑤

④ Enter the field after Green Lane and cross slightly R (80m). In the next field make for the far L corner (300m). In the 3rd field follow the curving L hedge to the end (250m). Cross the bridge to the next field and go on near the R edge to the narrow end (300m). Join Gay's Lane L and walk R past the little wood (100m).

⑤ Turn R along the end of the sports field near the wood (100m), R on the path at the corner (60m), L through the parking area to the corner (60m) then ahead through the passage way and along the next road (150m).

⑥ Turn R and continue along the drive to Stroud Farm (300m).

⑦ At the junction of farm tracks take the track L (100m). Cross the stream and turn R. Follow the path around outside the farm and pond (350m) then L away from the farm along the field boundaries (400m).

⑧ At the 4-way junction outside the large fields turn R. Keep on to the lane at Fifield (400m). Turn L to the village street (100m).

ⓔ *Little extension of 500m: Go L along the road to the end of the houses R (300m).*

ⓕ *Turn R on footpath outside the field initially (250m). Carry on in the field at the R hedge (250m), L&R behind the plantation (400m).*

ⓖ Cross the footbridge at the end and turn R into the adjacent field. Diverge from the L edge to the footbridge at the opposite edge (250m). Go straight across the next field (250m) and over the cross path into the next field. →⑪

⑨ Walk though the village R (250m) to Stewart Close R. (The **Fifield Inn** is 300m further on.)

⑩ Opposite Stewart Close take the path along the R edge of several fields to the first cross path (900m). Cross to the side field R.

⑪ Follow the L edge up to the road in Braywood (450m).

⑫ Walk R along the pavement until level with the middle of the cricket field (350m). Opposite, take the path L through the narrow fields (450m) and on up round L and R between fields (Windsor Castle far L) to Braywood House (450m). Skirt round the garden (100m) and turn R along the drive. Keep on to Drift Road opposite the gates of New Lodge (500m).

⑬ Follow the road R, towards Fifield Lane (700m).

~**field** is part of many village names locally: Fifield, Swallowfield, Warfield, Cruchfield, Englefield, Arborfield, Winkfield, Binfield, Shinfield. It derives from *feld*, in Saxon, a cleared area. Before Saxon colonization the district was densely wooded - later to be known as Windsor Forest. With new technology - plough teams of 6 or 8 oxen - the heavy soils on the London Clay could be cultivated and clearings appeared in the forest. The first part of the name may derive from the early owner or occupier of the clearing.

42 Cruchfield Manor and Paley Street

About 9¾ km/6 miles; gently undulating farmland; half shady in summer; avoid in wet seasons. OS maps 1:25000 160 Windsor, 1:50000 175 Reading.

Start from parking area at the end of Hawthorn Lane (a byway) beside the A330 100m east of Cruchfield Manor at Hawthorn Hill, SU 878 739.

Linking walks   38❖   39★   43✳

The Bridge House 01628 ☎ 623288

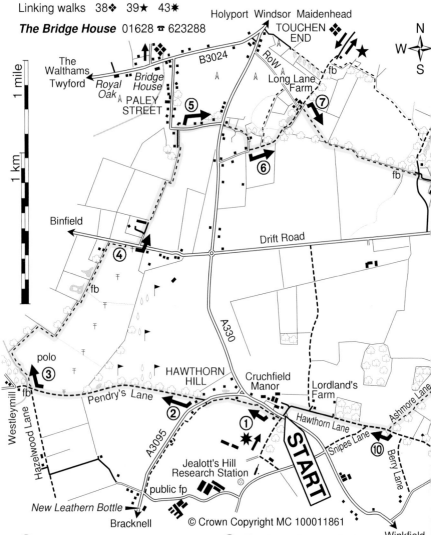

© Crown Copyright MC 100011861

① From the end of Hawthorn Lane cross the road and follow the horse track R beside it, past Cruchfield Manor opposite (150m) and round bends behind a house (200m) to the side track R (200m).

② The large house far L is Jealott's Hill. Cross the road and go down Pendry's Lane, a bridleway, beside the golf course (900m). Keep on between fields to the side path just before the ford (350m).

Red kites, *Milvus milvus*, were close to extinction in Britain with only a handful breeding in mid-Wales. Now they may be seen on every walk in this book. Being large and gyratory they are highly visible. The feature which distinguishes them is the chevron tail. The wings are fingered like buzzard's but have large pale patches. Kites are gregarious. They nest in trees often close to others and sometimes congregate in the air.

Reintroduction to England and Scotland began in 1989 with birds brought from Spain, Sweden and Germany. Counting ceased in 2005 but 320 pairs were estimated to have bred in the Chilterns area in 2006. Kites stay near their place of origin so the spread is slow as population density forces them apart. By 2013 they were nesting in woods on the Hampshire chalklands.

Dead pigeons and rabbits form most of their diet. They take live mice but are not good hunters. They scavenge in urban areas and in the middle ages were protected for their usefulness in cleansing towns of carrion.

③ Enter the field R and follow the edge beside the stream (250m). Go round the corner R and on along the hedge & ditch to the next corner (300m). Turn R again (100m) then L over the ditch. Carry on along the L hedge to the corner near Drift Road (700m).

④ Turn R along the edge of the field (100m) then join the road. Turn R beside it (100m) and take the farm drive L (150m). Stay ahead past the farm buildings to the field and along the R hedge (200m). At the end turn R into the adjacent field (25m) and follow the edge round L (250m) At the house cross to the drive and go down to the lane at the bend in Paley Street (100m). ❖

⑤ Turn R along the lane to the A330 (300m). Cross to the path beside the house. Carry on to the fields behind and beside the R hedge to the end (200m). Go R on the track and along the drive from the house to the R bend (100m).

⑥ Take the bridleway L between fields until level with the farmyard L at Long Lane Farm (500m). ★

⑦ Turn into the field R and cross obliquely towards the far R corner (300m). Just before it, enter the adjacent field R and follow the edge L to the byway (700m). Cross into the next field and go on along the track (100m). When it bends R, stay ahead over the fields to the path at the tree-lined edge (350m) and turn R to Drift Road (150m).

⑧ Go L along the road (200m) and take the byway R at the end of the field. Follow it between fields and up to the end of the wood. Watch out for the side path R just before the next field R (1000m). ✳

⑨ Follow the side path (Ashmore Lane) along the edge of the wood (150m) and continue between the fields to the byway (700m).

⑩ Turn R and follow the byway, Hawthorn Lane, to the end at the A330 (800m).

43 Warfield, Jealott's Hill and Hawthorn Hill

About 7¾ km/4¾ miles, with an extension of 2½ km/1½ miles; gently undulating farmland and lanes. OS maps 1:25000 160 Windsor,1:50000 175 Reading.

Start at the parking area opposite Warfield Church, SU 880 722, or at Frost Folly car park, SU 873 726, or at the parking area beside the A330 at the end of Hawthorn Lane near Cruchfield Manor at Hawthorn Hill, SU 878 739.

Linking walks   42✳   44✳

The Shepherds House ☎ 01344 423341
New Leathern Bottle ☎ 01344 421282

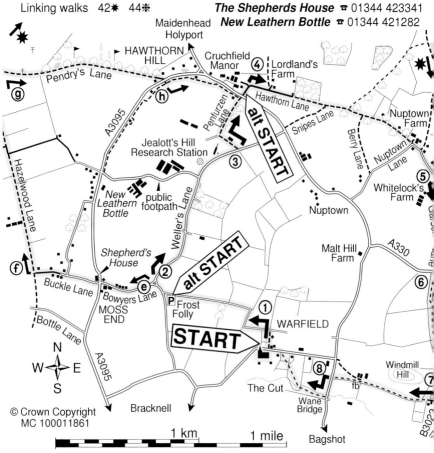

© Crown Copyright
MC 100011861

Walk around Warfield Church and back out to the road at the other churchyard gate (100m).

① Take the track L of the houses opposite the E gate (120m) and turn L on the concrete farm track between fields (200m). Go round R & L bends (150m) up to Frost Folly car park and the road (600m). Turn R to the 3-way junction (100m).

ⓔ *Extension of 2½ km/1½ miles: Turn L down to the A3095 opposite the **Shepherds House** (400m). Cross and go down Buckle Lane past the end of the tarmac (250m) to the track T-junction (150m).*

ⓕ *Turn R. Stay on this track past the next side track R (800m) to the end (off the map) near the ford and footbridge (600m).* ✳

(g) *Turn R. Stay ahead between fields then up past the golf course to the A3095 (1200m). Cross to the bridleway behind the trees.*

(h) *Follow the bridleway up L past Hawthorn Hill road junction to the end just after a house (600m).* ◆(4)

(2) Go R up Weller's Lane, past the side road L from Jealott's Hill Research Station (750m) and on.

(3) After the side road (350m) take the track L (250m). Go round the R bend and on under the trees to the A330 (300m). ✱ The large house 100m L is Cruchfield Manor.

(4) Cross to Hawthorn Lane (the byway) and walk away from the road, round the R bend (100m). Keep on to the tarmac at Nuptown Farm (1300m) and ahead to the next lane junction (400m). ✱

(5) Turn R. Follow Garson's Lane round L to the A330 (800m).

(6) Cross into the fields opposite and continue along the L edges to the end (650m) then L on the track to the road (100m) and R along the pavement (200m).

(7) Opposite the side road L, turn R along the stable drive (100m). Stay ahead between paddocks then along the L edge of the field to the barns of Apple Farm (600m). After the footbridge keep to the L hedge to the next lane (200m).

(8) Go down the lane L into the valley (150m). After Wane Bridge turn R. Cross a footbridge and follow the large brook (the Cut) into the corner of the next field (200m). Cross the footbridge and go up the field obliquely to the bottom corner of the garden. Continue on the same oblique line over the small fields to the road (250m). Turn L to Warfield Church (100m).

Warfield is not a nuclear village but a cluster of hamlets, a feature of forested land. One of the hamlets was Bracknell which became a New Town. The manor is WARFELT in the Domesday Book. After the Conquest it was crown land, royal demesne, having belonged to the queen of Edward the Confessor. The church, St Michael the Archangel, has a complex history. William the Conqueror presented its advowson to Geoffrey de Mandeville, who used it to endow his foundation of Hurley Priory. The monks provided the vicars. In 1391 they asked the king to be allowed to live at Warfield to escape Thames flooding which they blamed on the Templars' mill. The north aisle with Norman arches visible on the exterior was the 12th century nave. The Decorated north chapel was the 15th century chancel that had replaced the Norman sanctuary. The present chancel was the 14th century monks' chapel. The present nave was added in the 15th century. Of interest: Perpendicular rood screen of the north aisle with rood loft above; green man in the reredos; memorial to Thomas Williamson d1611 with his numerous children, Tudor porch, list of vicars. The external walls are puddingstone heathstone and flint; the internal, chalk and malmstone.

The Pish of Warfield & Easthampstead
Eileen Shorland 1980 Parish Council 106pp

Rectory House, behind the church, is the site of the medieval monks' living-quarters. From 1908 it was the home of William Herschal, 1833-1917, son and grandson of the astronomers. He was a very early exponent of colour photography and is credited with devising the principle of finger-printing. As a magistrate in India in 1858, he used palm prints for notarising contracts. (Finger-printing was put to forensic use by Henry Faulds, a missionary in Japan, and first accepted as evidence by a British court in 1905.)

Fingerprints - Murder and the Race to uncover the Science of Identity Beavan 2001 4th Estate

44 Winkfield and Maiden's Green

About 6 km/4 miles, with a short cut of ¾ km/½ mile; slightly undulating fields. Quite a lot of tarmac. OS maps 1:25000 160 Windsor, 1:50000 175 Reading.

Start at Winkfield Church, SU 904 723 (parking reserved during church functions)

Linking walk 43✳

The White Hart ☎ 01344 88241

Ⓢ *Short cut of 5 km/3miles: From Winkfield Church, facing the **White Hart**, turn R along the road (350m). Take the path L, between the first roadside houses (300m). Slightly L at the path junction after the mobile homes take the path ahead (300m), RLRL over streams (70m), on in the original direction (250m) then R to the houses (100m).* →③

① From Winkfield Church, cross to the **White Hart**, and go L along the pavement (200m). Opposite as St Mary's Lane L, take the path R between gardens and fields to the next road (400m). Follow the road R, on the L verge, down into the valley (350m).

② Just after the little bridge enter the field R. Walk along the R edge (350m), round the corner and along the end (250m). At the next corner cross the ditch to the field R and go on along L edge of several fields continuing on a cart track to the houses at Winkfield Row (600m).

③ Go L to the B3017 (200m) then R on the pavement up to the next road junction (600m). ✳

④ Follow the pavement R (200m). Opposite the farm drive take the side track L (100m). After the houses, enter the field R and go straight on along the edge to the next road (700m). Cross and follow Garson's Lane opposite (600m).

⑤ After Whitelock's Farm, pass the lane L and go on round R. Carry on to the next road (800m).

⑥ Cross to the pavement and go L, opposite the Old Forge, to the next road junction (200m).

⑦ Turn R into Winkfield Street (40m) then L between the gardens after the first house (80m). Go straight through the first field to a point just L of the far corner (100m). Carry on beside the L fence in the second field and into the third (200m). Bear R towards Winkfield church and pass through the churchyard to the road (250m).

The flat farmland around Winkfield and Holyport is on the London Clay outcrop between the Chiltern chalk and the heap of Tertiary Sands under Bagshot Heath and Camberley. With the right amount of rain you may get feet of clay and annoy the locals by stamping it off on their tarmac drives, pavements and roads. From many of the walks in this book the Tertiary Sands are visible as an eminence to the south. The Look Out is on its north edge at Bracknell.

People seem to think of the London Clay as a layer of soil but it is a stratum up to 300' thick which is unlithified (ie not turned to rock). It accumulated on the sinking sea bed 60 million years

The Chilterns are the chalk outcrop emerging from the great syncline of the London Basin. Beyond the area of this book they peak at 267m/870'. The land is dissected everywhere by deep valleys, almost all dry. The rain which falls now is able to drain away through the very porous chalk and the valleys are generally attributed to the much heavier rainfall before and after the several glaciations of the Ice Age. Steepness prevents ploughing so the fields are mostly used for grazing despite excellent fertile soil.

Most of the Chiltern chalk is covered by Pleistocene (Ice Age) deposits with belts of gravel probably formed as

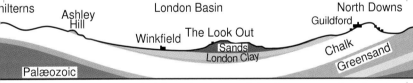

ago during the Eocene period. Its palm seed and crocodile fossils suggest the climate was warmer then but Winkfield was also a bit closer to the equator. Soils upon the London Clay tend to be clayey but soil creep down slopes and flood deposits ensure not all the soils are clayey. The tiny particles have very fine spaces between them which grip water excluding air. Soil microbes and roots need oxygen so the farmland has numerous deep drainage ditches to let the water drop out of the surface layer making space for air. The upper slopes may grow cereals but lower slopes are suitable only for pasture so grazing has come to predominate - mostly horses now. This land was Windsor Forest.

outwash by the torrents of melt water. Blown silt (loess) deposited during arid frozen periods, became the brick-earths used at the Pinkneys tile- and brickworks. These deposits often form soils too low in pH for cultivation or pasture so they are wooded with birch and may have small patches of heath or conifer plantations. Some of the hilltops are muddy even in summer. This is attributed to *clay with flints*, a layer thought to be formed from fine particles remaining when the calcium carbonate of the chalk dissolves plus ice age dust. The clay is uneconomic to plough so these hills are capped by woods which provide scenery, timber, pheasants and nest sites for kites.

Ashley Hill, 475', is an outlier of Reading Beds and London Clay on the Chalk, rising towards the Chilterns. The Reading Beds are a highly fossiliferous layer of beach deposits of Eocene age below the London Clay.

Aston is a hamlet of Remenham. The lane down through it led to a rope ferry.

BCA, Berkshire College of Agriculture started in 1949. It has moved into allied areas: equestrian, veterinary nursing, horticulture, conservation, floristry and cemetery operatives' training and serves as local technical college with motor engineering, childcare, sports courses and academic sciences.

Bisham was BISTESHÃ in the Domesday Book, taxed for 12 arpents of vines but no eels. The Norman lord of the manor, Henry de Ferrers, had been one of the Domesday Book surveyors. In 1138 his descendent gave the estate to the Knights Templar who built a preceptory. After the Templars were suppressed in 1307 the Earl of Salisbury acquired it and founded a priory of Austin canons in 1337. The Salisbury family tomb is there, position unknown, with Warwick the Kingmaker. Henry VIII made it into a Benedictine house, his only monastic foundation, but dissolved it 7 months later. Subsequent owners have been the Hobys and Vansittarts. The "Abbey" has been a place of some importance. Robert the Bruce's wife, Elizabeth was kept there. Queen Mary kept her sister Elizabeth there for a short period. The house, Bisham Abbey, was built in 1560 round the Templars' hall. This is now the National Sport Centre.

Bisham Woods is a modern name for several woods owned by the Woodland Trust along the chalk escarpment. At the northern end is Quarry Wood.

Bolney was BOLLEHEDE in the Oxfordshire folios of the Domesday Book. It probably never had a village and is now part of Harpsden parish.

Boulter's Lock was the lowest of the pound locks, built for the Commissioners in 1772. It was then against the Taplow Bank but moved to the Berkshire side in 1811. It has been rebuilt several times and is the largest lock above Teddington. Freight through it was 69,285 tons p.a. for 1785-92. The last salmon caught there was in 1811. The mill belonged to the Ray family in the 14th century. Ray Mill Island is now a pleasure garden owned by the borough.

Bourne End is a 20th century town based on one of the ancient hamlets of Wooburn Parish. The railway, arriving in 1854, provided a nucleus but the rapid growth was in the 1950s and 60s. The name would derive from Wye Bourne, which enters the Thames downriver of the railway bridge. Edgar Wallace lived here. The Fire Fly was a GWR Gooch engine, 2-2-2, which did 50mph in 1840.

Boveney is two small manors written BOUENIÆ and BOUENIE in the Buckinghamshire folios of the Domesday Book. One was given to Burnham Abbey in 1266. The chapel, St Mary Magdalene, is obscure in its origin. It may have been the parish church when Boveney was a larger village. It has 13th century features and may be earlier. The *ey* sound in Bov*ey*, Boln*ey*, *E*ton and Dorn*ey* derives from the Saxon for island. Presumably these places were on hard ground in the original marsh or between braids of the untamed river.

Boveney Ditch is now the boundary between Berkshire and Buckinghamshire. The southern tip (Slough and Eton) was transferred to Berkshire in 1974.

Boveney Lock was here before 1375 for a City of London letter book records a dispute over Baddebyeloke tolls. It belonged to John Baddeby and would have been a flash lock. Gill's Bucks were here and probably older. The first pound lock of 1838 was in the ditch beside the present lock.

Bovingdon Green, a hamlet of Marlow, was Buvendon in 1263 possibly from the Saxon *bufan dune*, above the hill.

Bray is BRAI in the Domesday Book, a Royal Hundred and the address of two manors. The village may have been initiated by the building of the medieval church but the Saxon town may have been Holyport. The oldest pottery in Britain, dated to 3340BC, was found on the Binghams estate. Oldfield was the archery butts and venue in 1773 for the first recorded Berkshire cricket match. The church, St Michael, built in 1293, is a splendid large village church, with flint and clunch walls and a castellated tower acting as porch. Bits of the 13th century fabric remain but there has been extensive re-building, often copying the original. The chantry chapel, on the north side of the churchyard, may be late 13th century and held the 18th century free school. The 15th century gate house may have been the chantry house. Bray's renown comes from the song *The Vicar of Bray* said to be written by an officer of Colonel Fuller's Regiment at the time of George I. The song does not accord with church records which show a succession of three vicars during the period of religious vacillation.

The Royal Hundred of Bray L Over & C Tyrrell 1993 Cliveden Press 144p

Bray Lock was built "without sides" in 1844.

Braywood House was a vicarage and has the graveyard of All Saints Church as its garden. The church was built by Mrs Van der Weyer of New Lodge in 1866 allowing Bray parish to be subdivided but was demolished around 1960.

Buckinghamshire is Bochinghamscire in the Domesday Book but does not appear in the Anglo-Saxon Chronicles from the 7th century onwards. It may have been a new creation on the edge of the Danelaw to sustain the burhs placed at Buckingham by Edward the Elder in 914. The *Tribal Hidage*, probably drafted in 7th century Mercia, has a Chiltern people, the Ciltern Sætna, listed for 4000 hides. It is unclear whether they were celtic natives or continental.

Clewer was CLIVORE in the Domesday Book, a manor rated at 5 hides but with half a hide deducted for the castle. In the 1316 tax returns it was the Borough of (New) Windsor. St Andrews' church is mostly of 1850 re-building but the south chapel and aisle and the tower date from around 1180. The grave of Daniel Gooch the great GWR locomotive engineer is in the churchyard.

Cliveden is now a hotel leased from the National Trust. The grounds are open to the public (NT ☎ 01628 605069). The present house of 1851 is on land of the medieval de Clyveden family. The first house of note here was built in 1666 for George Villiers, 2nd Duke of Buckingham, the richest man in England at the time and the B in CABAL. He had a terrace cut out of the hilltop to give the house a view the river and to let it be viewed. It is best known as the home of the Astor family in the 20th century, Nancy Astor being the first women MP to take her seat. *The Cliveden set* was a term of disparagement when they were perceived as Nazi appeasers.   *Cliveden* J Crathorne 1995 Collins & Brown 224pp

Cock Marsh is common land of Cookham and Maidenhead Hundred. It has been owned by the National Trust since 1934. Commoners still graze cattle in the summer; up to 100 appear. The fertile flood plains round about have long been settled and the mound in Cock Marsh is a Bronze age barrow - jaw bone was found in it in 1874 and the remains of a Saxon warrior and his dog.

Cookham is pleasant for strolling by the Thames. It was the birthplace and haunt of Stanley Spencer, the painter. The name first appears as COCCHAM in a charter of around 798 which also indicates there was a monastery founded at the beginning of that century. Cookham was sometimes in the kingdom of Wessex and sometimes in Mercia. A Saxon owner willed the manor to King Edgar in the 960s and it remained a Crown Estate until 1818. Æthelred the Unred held a Witan here in 996. In the Domesday Book, COCHEHÃ was a large manor rated for 20 hides, 100 pigsworth of woodland and two mills.

Cookham Church, Holy Trinity, may be on the site of the Domesday Book church but the earliest fabric is Norman; the nave dates from about 1140. Churchgate House was built around 1350 and has been the residence of the Abbots of Cirencester who were the rectors. Overy's Farm in the High Street is of the same age. *Bel & the Dragon* is a late 15th century house. The *Kings Arms* was the coaching inn. The Tarrystone is a sarsen and was probably a boundary stone but has been moved about; in 1506 the warrener was criticised for not holding sports at it. Moor Place, built in 1805, was used as the Gaumont-British cartoon film studio during World War II.

Cookham Bridge replaced a ferry. It was built in timber in 1840 by a company set up for the purpose and rebuilt in cast iron 30 years later. The two counties adopted it in 1947. The toll house is still there, at the Buckinghamshire end.

Cookham Dean probably derives its name from the Saxon *dene*, valley, but it might come from the Dean of Cirencester who owned some of the land. The village is a delightful, chaotic jumble of houses, lanes, greens and dry valleys, in part of the Chilterns cut off by the Thames. It acquired its centre relatively recently with the establishment of the church, St John the Baptist in 1844, apparently to curb the lawlessness of the dwellers in the Thicket and Bisham Woods. *The Royal Hundred of Cookham* L Over & C Tyrrell 1994 Cliveden Press 143pp

Cranbourne Tower, a remnant of Cranbourne Lodge built about 1500, has been a residence for royal family and government officials. Pepys recorded his visits to Sir George Carteret (Treasurer to the Navy) and in 1666 writes of burnt paper falling during the Fire of London. Eclipse, the racehorse and sire to pubs of that name, was foaled here in 1764 in the Duke of Cumberland's stables. *The Story of Windsor Great Park* R J Elliott Crown Estate Commissioners

Cruchfield Manor house on Hawthorn Hill is Georgian Classical of around 1800. The estate probably corresponds to the smaller manor of Bray rated at 1 hide in the Domesday Book. It was KERCHESFELD in 1185 and rated at 1 hide when Henry Lovell owned it in 1272. The Close Roll for 1286 calls Cruchefend a vaccaria in the forest (cow farm). Archæological excavation in 1991 suggests it was surrounded by a very early village, cleared around 1485.

Culham Court, a splendid Georgian mansion on a splendid site, was built in 1771. The estate was part of the Domesday Book manor of Wargrave but detached, probably in the 13th century. The earliest document is a quitclaim obtained by the landowner, the Bishop of Winchester, from Edward I in 1284.

Cumberland Lodge since 1947 has been the home of the St Catherine's Foundation inspired by Amy Buller (1891-1974) for students and professionals to meet and exchange ideas. The first house was built around 1650 by John Byfield, a Roundhead officer, who bought 700 acres after the execution of Charles I. Grooms House may be the farm house from that time. After the Restoration, when Charles II bought back the park, it became the Ranger's Lodge for Bab May. Under Queen Anne, the Marlboroughs were joint Rangers; the Duchess, Sarah Churchill, was thwarted here in her plan to marry a grand daughter, Lady Diana Spencer, to the Prince of Wales. George II's son, William Augustus, Duke of Cumberland, became Ranger in 1746. A major-general at 21 and victor of Culloden, he inspired Handel's Opera *Judas Maccabæus (See the Conquering Hero Come)* and the nick-name "Butcher Bill". He employed his soldiers to dam and dig Virginia Water and the Obelisk Pond. Prince Christian of Schleswig-Holstein was the last Ranger to live here, husband of Helena, Queen Victoria's third daughter. In 1936, the decision to oppose Edward VIII's marriage to Mrs Simpson was taken at Cumberland Lodge. *Cumberland Lodge* Helen Hudson 1997 Phillimore 236pp

The **Cut** collects up numerous springs and drainage ditches in Binfield and becomes the waterway which makes Bray an island, opening to the Thames near Bray Marina. It runs mainly in straight lines testifying to its artificiality.

Danesfield was completed in 1901, on the site of earlier large houses, by R W Hudson, son of the Sunlight soap magnate. During World War II it was requisitioned as RAF Medmenham for Air Intelligence (Reconnaissance & Photography); it processed 36m photos. Later it was bought by the Air Ministry for the HQ of 90 Group (Signals). Carnation Milk acquired it as company HQ in 1977. Since 1991 it has been a luxury hotel. There are prehistoric fortifications around the 20 acre site and it is reputed to have been a Viking camp.

The **deer fence** dates from 1979. The present herd of red deer was started in 1979 with stock from Scotland and is kept at 600 for self sufficiency in the 1000 acre enclosure; they are fed only under extreme conditions. New animals have been introduced many times but the original Great Park would have been enclosed for hunting indigenous deer. Few survived the civil war when Windsor was a Roundhead garrison town and the Great Park was broken up. The rut, when the stags roar and fight, is October-November; calves are seen in June.

Dorney is DORNEI in Burnham Hundred in the Buckinghamshire folios of the Domesday Book. It had no mill but a fishery that was taxed @ 500 eels. The church, St James the Less, is 12th century or earlier, altered little since the 14th century. Features of interest: the splendid late 16th century Garrard tomb; the priest's door with a window arch outside in the south wall, possibly Saxon.

Dorney Court is open to the public. It is the present manor house, a fine timber-framed house of about 1510. It has been in the Palmer family since 1530 and kept in excellent condition. One of the Palmers, against advice, married Barbara Villiers, later the notorious Countess of Castlemaine, mistress of Charles II. The first pineapple in Britain was grown here in 1665 and also went to the king. The adjacent garden centre serves lunches and cream teas.

The **Dorney Lake** of Eton College is one of our main national rowing venues hosting the World Rowing Championships in 2006 and the Olympics in 2013. It is 2000m long and wide enough for 8 rowing lanes. The Boathouse has the facilities for large rowing events and is available as a conference centre. The park surrounding the lake has paths and cycleways open to the public.

Dorneywood is sometimes in the news because of its occupant. It was left to the nation in 1947 by Lord Courtauld-Thompson to be the official residence of a senior member of government. It is a Queen Anne house in 215 acres.

Down Place is the 1750s mansion where the Kit-Kat Club met. It is now Bray Studios of the Hammer horror films. The Kit Kat Club was an early 18th century clique of leading Whig politicians and writers possibly initiated for the ousting of James II and support of William of Orange. Kneller was a member and painted the portraits of all the members. The house is at Water Oakley, a hamlet of Bray parish. A large Roman cemetery was uncovered at gravel works nearby.

Dunsden is DUNESDENE in the Domesday Book, a manor of 20 hides of the Bishop of Salisbury. The parish is long and narrow down to the Thames like its neighbours. The 150' well on the green was the gift of benefactors in 1878.The church was built a mile from the Green in 1842. Wilfred Owen was the priest's assistant for two years before WWI which made him famous and dead.

Eton was ETTONE in Burnham Hundred in the Buckinghamshire folios of the Domesday Book. Before the Conquest it belonged to the queen; afterwards to Walter son of Othere, castellan of Windsor and founder of the great medieval family of the name; its tax rating included 1000 eels and 20s for 2 mills.

Eton College is open to visitors at certain times. The college buildings line the roads of Eton. Numerous public footpaths cross the playing fields and walkers wander where there is no right of way. The college was founded by Henry VI in 1442, to provide a chantry for his soul, an alms-house and a school for 25 poor and indigent scholars... neither villeins nor bastards ... ie sons of local middle class parents. The scholars soon became 70 and additional boys could pay to live in (commensales) or lodge in the town (oppidans) to take lessons. The original training was solely workday Latin to fit the boys for employment as clerks. After the Restoration, aristocratic oppidans joined and the Latin became classical. In the middle of the 19th century the independent lodgings became houses of the college, maths was introduced, the scholarship system eliminated poor boys and most of the buildings took on their present form. Black dress was adopted by the boys in mourning for George III and has remained ever since. 5660 old Etonians served in the Great War and 1157 died, a few being on the other side. Eton chapel which can be seen from afar, was built 1443-76, a fine example of perpendicular style but now with a fake roof. Lupton's Tower, early 16th century, can be seen through the main portal behind the statue of Henry VI the founder. The Long Chamber in which all 70 early scholars were locked at night is the upper part of the building adjacent to the drive gate - one of the earliest brick buildings in Britain.   *Eton* Christopher Hollis 1960 Hollis & Carter 332pp

Eton Wick is largely composed of modern houses but there are a few ancient houses on the north side eg Bell Farm built before 1400. *Wick*, in thousands of British place-names, is cognate with *vicus*, Latin for village or hamlet. It may have been appended to distinguish the village from the manor.

Fawley Court is said to be the inspiration for Toad Hall of *Wind in the Willows*. Until 2008 it belonged to the Marian Fathers, who originated in Poland in 1673. It is now a private residence. The house was built 1684-88 by Sir Christopher Wren for Sir William Freeman. It has a ceiling carved by Grindling Gibbon. The park was laid out in 1771 by Capability Brown. Temple Island was part of the grounds, the temple being a folly. Bulstrode Whitlocke had a house on the site destroyed in 1642 by the Royalists under Sir John Byron. Fawley village is two miles away from the river. The manor is FALELEI in the Domesday Book.

Fifield is a hamlet of Bray, a ribbon development of mainly modern houses between two main roads. Some of the surrounding farm houses and cottages are of interest. Yew Tree Cottage dates from about 1550 and its internal structures shows that it was a hall house.

Flemish Farm, beside Windsor Great Park, was developed by George III for personal interest and experimentation, hence his nick-name "Farmer George". It used the Flemish system of crop rotation in contrast to Norfolk Farm.

Foliejon Park is a private residence in 500 acres. The estate was given by Edward I in 1302 to John of Drokensford, a court official who went on to be the Bishop of Bath & Wells. Edward II confiscated it to discharge the bishop's debts and *Folly John* appears to be a nickname from that time. Thereafter it was granted to a succession of royal officials and, being under the eye of royal clerks of works, became the subject of many extant medieval documents. Charles I sold it when his lack of parliaments caused his want of money, since when it has sometimes been called Winkfield Park. It has passed through many families, memorialized in Winkfield Church. The present house was built about 1800. King Haakon of Norway lived here during his exile in World War II. Mining & Chemical Products Ltd used it as company HQ and laboratories in the 1950s & 60s. The ornamental gatehouse was built in 1997.

Foliejon Park W J Morris & M Crosland Mining & Chemical Products 1970

Greenlands is now the Henley Management College. W H Smith owned the Hambleden estate and lived there. The WHS logo appears on estate houses.

Hall Place is now an admin building of Berkshire College of Agriculture. It is on the site of the medieval manor house of Hurley, La Halle. After John Lovelace built the new manor house, *Ladye Place*, in the village, Hall Place had a succession of owners. Some of the present features, eg Diana the Huntress statue, were placed here by Joseph Bancks late in the 17th century but the present house was completed in 1735 for William East, a London lawyer. The interior is fairly austere but the drawing room, now used as the college staff room, has stucco portraits of Anne, daughter of George II, and William, Prince of Orange, whose marriage cemented the enduring alliance of their nations. The East family had the house until 1939. It was requisitioned for the wartime HQ of Trinidad Lake Asphalt, now the multinational company Tarmac.

Hambleden is HANBLEDENE in the Domesday Book, a riparian manor taxed for 1000 eels and a mill. The village is small and picturesque. The parish had a population of 970 in 1794 and is about 1800 now. Kenricks, the Georgian house on the hillside, is the former rectory. The Manor House near the church is Jacobean, built 1603. Several eminent men originated here. The best known son of Hambleden is James Thomas Brudenell 1793-1868, who led the charge of the Light Brigade, 1854 and gave his name to a woolly garment. Thomas de Cantilupe, 1218-88, Chancellor of England and Bishop of Worcester was born here and canonised 1320. *Hambleden* is a toponym: *hamble* from broken country, *dene* valley. The church, St Mary the Virgin, is cruciform, the oldest part being the arcade of the north transept, of around 1230, inserted when the church was a 100 years old. Points of interest: the font which may be Saxon, the reusable stone coffin in the north transept, the alabaster memorial to Sir Cope D'Oyley, the church chest which was Lord Cardigan's army box, many brasses and the 16th century elaborately carved Wolsey altar in the S transept.

A **Hambleden Weir** would have powered the Domesday Book mill. Edward III received complaints in 1376 about a lock called Hamelden newly rebuilt whereat boatmen had been in great peril...and one lately perished. The pound lock of 1773 was one of the first eight ordered by the Thames commissioners. The weir was last rebuilt in 1996. The walkway along the weir is a public footpath. The mill used to supply flour for Huntley & Palmers in Reading. When it closed in 1958 it had been milling cattle food. It is now apartments.

Harleyford Manor House, a palladian red-brick residence, architect Sir Robert Taylor, was built soon after 1755; the previous house was demolished because of Civil War damage. The manor came about through subinfeudation of Great Marlow Manor and was eventually purchased back into it. Sir Miles Hobart of Harleyford is said to be the MP who locked Charles I out of the Commons.

Harpsden was HARPENDENE in the Oxfordshire section of the Domesday Book. The village, never large, is now two clusters of houses. The parish in the shape of the original manor is a long strip from the Thames to the top of the chalk. The church, St Margaret, is mainly Victorian Gothic but Norman fragments remain: the south doorway, piscina and font. There are several brasses. The earliest record of a rector is in 1218. The sheds opposite the church are curiosities for their cladding of wall-paper printing blocks.

Hedsor is a hilltop village without a nucleus. In the Curia Regis Rolls for 1195 it was Heddesore which might derive from an owner called Hædda and *ofer*, cliff. The church, St Nicholas, is a 12th century foundation but the earliest fabric is 15th century. Church Path in Woolman's Wood may be the Roman road. Hedsor Wharf was the name of a house and estate as well as a port.

Henley, Oxfordshire, is not in the Domesday Book and owes its development wholly to the river. It is now universally associated with the rowing regatta but in the middle ages was the terminus for the largest barges as well as having a bridge. Almost the entire population was wharfingers and barge operators in the 18th century. The regatta started in 1839, originally in Remenham, and the Leander Club is the senior world rowing institution. Henley Reach is an almost straight mile where the racing takes place with the temple as starting point.

Henley Bridge opened in 1778, the previous one having fallen in the flood of 1774 and an earlier one being destroyed in the Civil War. The earliest evidence for a bridge is an order of 1231 to cart oaks for it from Windsor Forest.

Holyport has a picturesque village green surrounded by quaint houses, some ancient. On the green, *Hamble Cottage* may be 14th century. *Duel's House* and *Coventry Cottage* are 15th century. *Goff's Cottage*, *The Rails* and *The George* are 16th. Holyport is an important component of Bray Parish and may well be the original village of the Domesday Book since it lies in the centre of the Hundred and has a Saxon name (*port* denoting a market) in contrast to *Bray* which is thought to be Norman. It had several small medieval holdings corresponding to the men-at-arms' holdings of the Bray entry in the Domesday Book. The Real Tennis Club in Holyport Street, apparently a Queen Anne house, was built in 1889 with innovatory panels for the playing walls and floor.

Hurley's last Saxon lord of the manor was Edward the Confessor's Master of Horse, Asgar. He was injured and survived the Battle of Hastings but was stripped of his estates. Geoffrey de Mandeville, a companion of William the Conqueror, was awarded Hurley and many other manors in 11 counties. In the Domesday Book HERLEI was assessed for 13¾ hides, 2 fisheries and a church. Knowl Hill, Burchett's Green, Cockpole, Warren Row and part of Littlewick belong to the original manor and parish. The village always had good communications because of the river and, from the end of the 18th century, the Henley-Maidenhead turnpike road. When the GWR came to Maidenhead in 1839, 5 miles by pony and trap, Hurley became fashionable. Ye Olde Bell Inn originated in 1135 as a guesthouse for the priory. A bell was rung to inform the denizens of the arrival of an important visitor. The present building dates from just before 1500. The last Oxford coach called in 1890. The priory church was consecrated in 1086, the year the Domesday Book was compiled, but the present church, St Mary, is late 12th century in style. Much of the fabric is original but the odd windows are later replacements or insertions.

Hurley Priory was founded by Geoffrey de Mandeville in memory of his first wife. It was a cell of the Benedictine Westminster Abbey which still holds the founding charter of 1086. The buildings form the nucleus of the present village around the church but little remains of the domestic parts. The refectory is the building parallel with the church in the quadrangle and the monks' stone barn is still prominent in the High Street. In 1255 the priory was in litigation with the Knights Templar downstream whose weir they blamed for flooding. Being worth only £121 18s 5d, Hurley Priory was in the first wave of dissolutions in 1536. Henry VIII gave the estate to Westminster Abbey in exchange for the Covent Garden but then dissolved that Abbey two years later. The 562 documents of the Priory held at Westminster Abbey were published by a Victorian vicar, providing vignettes of the life, economy and events in medieval times.

Hurley Lock was built in 1773, the fifth of the Thames Commissioners' first eight pound locks. The toll was 1d per ton of freight in 1793. The owners of the (flash) lock in 1580 are recorded as Mr Bowde & Mr Lovelace. Across the river is a restored winch which was used to pull vessels up through the flash lock.

Hurst was the name of the Manor of Whistley when handed over by Abingdon Abbey to Henry VIII in 1538. The church, St Nicholas, has a fluted capital of about 1180 in the north arcade, the oldest datable fabric. The north doorway is 13th century; roof timbers 15th century; pulpit Jacobean; the lancet windows Victorian; 3-stage brick tower 1612. One of the table tombs is for Thomas Dundas, a Trafalgar captain. The almshouses opposite the church were built in 1664 as a hospital for the maintenance of 8 poor persons each at 6 pence per diem for ever. The present village is mainly modern houses near Twyford.

Jealott's Hill Research Station came into existence when ICI bought the estate for their first agricultural chemicals research centre in 1928. It continued under the subsequent companies, Zeneca and Syngenta. Pesticides and herbicides are developed and assessed in laboratory and field for efficacy and hazards. New varieties are produced and tested. The glass houses test tropical crops. The fields around are farmed commercially by the company.

The **Jubilee River** is an artificial cut for flood relief across a loop of the Thames, 12km/7½ miles long from Taplow to Datchet. It was completed in 2002, the Golden Jubilee year of Elizabeth II, The main control is the sluice beside Taplow Mill but it has other weirs to retain water for habitat protection.

Knowl Hill was a hamlet of Hurley but became a separate parish in 1842. The clay pit was used for brick making. The church, St Peter's, was built in 1842 by the architect J C Butler. The name appears to be a dilingual repetition.

Ladye Place in Hurley has a place in English history as the venue in 1688 for plotting the Glorious Revolution by John Lovelace III and friends. James II was ousted without bloodshed and William of Orange invited to take the throne. Ladye Place was the manor house. The medieval mansion was pulled down in 1838 and the name transferred to the farmhouse. This was HQ for US Naval Intelligence in World War II. The original mansion was built by John Lovelace I who bought the estate in 1543 soon after the priory was dissolved. It was SE of the church and remains in the churchyard wall. The monks' tithe barn, in the grounds, dates from about 1350. The dovecot has 750 niches and dates from around 1300. A deed of 1396 shows the prior gave John Terry an annual pension of 30s plus 200 pigeons which would have come from this dovecote.

Littlewick Green has a delightful village cricket green. The area was part of Domesday Book Hurley but was populous enough to have its own church in 1887. Ivor Novello lived at Redroofs from 1928 until he died in 1951.

Littleworth Common is heath on Ice Age deposits over chalk. Beside it is Dropmore Church, St Anne, of 1865. The parish and hamlet took the name of the church which took its name from the Dropmore estate when the owner carved it out of the woods in 1792. He was William Wyndham, later Lord Grenville who led the *ministry of all the talents* at the time of George III.
Dropmore & Littleworth, story of a South Bucks parish 1996 Burnham Historians 233pp

The River **Loddon**, flows from chalk springs in the middle of Basingstoke, collects the ancient Blackwater from the Surrey border and debouches through several channels into the Thames between Sonning and Wargrave.

Maidenhead is ELENTONE in the Domesday Book, a small manor between the two large royal manors, Bray and Cookham. It was South Ellington until the end of the 13th century. A moated site in North Town, probably a manor house, excavated in 1966 & 72, yielded 2 tons of 13-15th century pottery. The 13th century bridge deflected the Great West Road (A4) from its ford at Cookham allowing Maidenhead to eclipse its neighbours. The GWR made it fashionable and put it into the commuter belt. *The Story of Maidenhead* Luke Over MRM 1984 63pp

Maidenhead Bridge was built in stone in 1777 beside an earlier timber bridge. The earliest reference is Henry III's order to widen the road between Henley and Maidenhead Bridge in 1255. Pontage was 1d in 1337 for each loaded cart over and loaded vessel under: for navigators bridges are obstructions.

Little Marlow is a small village with two pubs. The church, St John the Baptist, has a round Norman arch in the chapel; the chancel arch, though pointed antedates 1100. There was a 12th century nunnery which owned the manor. In 1534 it was valued at £21 3s 7d pa and wound up. The land was given to Bisham Abbey just before the Dissolution; the buildings disappeared.

Marlow is a thriving town enclosed by the foothills of the Chilterns but always linked to the outer world, and latterly fashionable, because of the Thames. The medieval centre and church were at the wharf but growth was up the healthier slopes. The Domesday Book manor, MERLAUE, later called Great Marlow, was in Desborough Hundred - one of the three Chiltern Hundreds. Townsmen had burghage rights in 1183 but most of the documents plotting the town's history have been lost. Marlow burned in 1644 during the Civil War. After his grand tour of Britain in 1708 Defoe wrote: Marlow is a town of great Embarkation on the Thames, not so much for goods wrought here (for the trade of the town is chiefly in bone lace) ..... a very great quantity of malt and meal is brought hither from High Wyckham ... and loaded on the barges for London. The suspension bridge of 1832 replaced earlier timber bridges. The town church, All Saints, was built in 1832 on the site of the medieval church whose memorials it displays. Marlow Place, at the top of St Peter's Street, a baroque house of 1690-1720, was occupied by George II as Prince of Wales. Early in the 19th century it was a hostel for the army college. Sir William Borlase's Grammar School was founded in 1624 to teach 24 poor boys to read, write and cast accounts and 24 girls to knit, spin and make bone lace. Nearby, at 104, the Shelleys lived for a year, 1817-18; Mary Shelley completed *Frankenstein* here. Remnantz, a fine 18th century house, was the Royal Military College from 1799 until it moved to Sandhurst in 1812. Court Garden house in the park is said to be the source of the expression "batty". It was designed about 1750 by a Dr Battie who forgot to put in a staircase.

Marlow Lock had a winch in 1306. The old flash lock caused many deaths. The pound lock opened in 1773, the 7th of the original eight. Toll records show 56,354 tons of up-river freight passed through in 1767. There was no towing path between the bridge and the lock and towlines of ¼ mile had to be used. Marlow Mill was producing paper in 1865.

Marsh Lock is approached by a towpath over the water. Sir John Drayton of Rotherfield Peppard was indicted in 1403 for not keeping the lock and winch in good repair. There were two mills in 1585. One of the new pound locks opened here in 1773 and was re-built in 1787. The toll was 1d per ton in 1793. A report of 1794 indicates there were two corn mills on the Berkshire side and a corn and paper mill on the Oxfordshire side and two sets of bucks.

Medmenham is a village on the steep valley side of the Thames with large houses and ancient cottages in flint. It was the Domesday Book manor of MEDEMEHAM which William the Conqueror took from the Saxon freeman Wulfstan and kept for himself. The first Norman Lord of the Manor, Hugh de Bolebec lived in a castle of which only the outer earthwork is now visible on the hillside above the church. The church, SS Peter & Paul, was founded by the Lord of the Manor, Hugh Bolebec II, 1100-65, but has been altered in many later styles. Points of interest: original Norman south doorway (inside porch); the tie beam instead of a chancel arch, chequer board wall of clunch and flint; the hatchment of Ann Danvers, daughter of Sir William Borlase.

Medmenham Abbey is an old house said to have been a venue of the Hell Fire Club though *Victoria County History* disputes this. Sir Francis Dashwood, Chancellor of the Exchequer lived there and, around 1743, inaugurated the "Knights of St Francis of Wycombe", a spoof title for his clique of opposition politicians, lampooned as the Mad Monks of Medmenham. The house is on the site of a Cistercian abbey which was endowed in 1201 in the reign of Stephen by Hugh de Bolebec and dissolved in 1536. The monks came from Woburn.

Monkey Island is said to derive its name from Monks Eyot (islet). It was used for fishing by monks of Merton Priory which had a cell at Amerden Bank. Later it was owned by Burnham Abbey. After the Fire of London masonry rubble was dumped on it and other islands. The Duke of Marlborough bought the island in 1738 and built splendid fishing lodges which, by stages, turned into the hotel.

New Lodge is offices but has been a Barnado's home and a catering school for British Rail. The Victorian Gothic house was built in 1857 as a gift for the Belgian Ambassador, Jan Silvain van der Weyer, by his American father-in-law. It is on the site of a keeper's cottage in Windsor Forest at the time of James I. The tower has radio and light beacons for Heathrow.

Oakley Court is at Water Oakley, a hamlet of Bray. It was built in 1859 but had several owners - one was Sir William Avery of the scales - before it became a hotel in 1981. It is said to have been the HQ of the French Resistance. Bray Studios arose in the adjacent grounds of Down Place in 1955 and used Oakley Court in many films including *St Trinians*, *Half a Sixpence* and *Dracula*.

Ockwells Manor was the ancestral estate of the Norreys family, probably in origin, a purpestre around 1255 in the Royal Manor of Bray; in 1284 Richard le Norreys was paying 3d for the pastorage of cattle in the frith. The house was built for John Norreys around 1450 so it is pre-Tudor. It has many of its original features, including the armorial glass in the hall window apparently to celebrate the marriage treaty of Henry VI to Margaret of Anjou (1445). John Norreys (d 1466) and his son (d 1506) are cited by *The Oxford History of England* as secular medieval civil servants who retained authority throughout the Wars of the Roses. They served four kings (Henry VI, Edward IV, Richard III & Henry VII) and survived three usurpations, presumably because they were valued for their skills and were politically benign or flexible.

The **Old Forge** has the previous church clock and is inscribed "Henry Druce, maker 1698". Church records show the blacksmith made it here for the church on condition he was paid 40s p.a. for winding it (early form of hire purchase?).

Philberds, at Holyport, was the home of Nell Gwyn and her son, the Duke of St Albans, but all that is left is a moat at the end of Holyport Street. The estate derived from one of the smaller Domesday Book holdings of Bray. The last big house was demolished in 1919 after being a German officer POW camp.

Pinkneys Green is the area of housing estates on the edge of Maidenhead as well as the area of grass, cut by roads. The name derives from the French owner after the Conquest of Elentone Manor on which Maidenhead arose. In the Domesday Book this is Giles, a native of Picquigny in Picardy. The trees north of the main green hide the extensive pits of the Brick & Tile works which closed in the 1980s - now a National Trust site. When Camley Gardens estate was built in 1964, 11 medieval pottery kilns were found, exploiting the clay.

Railways: see summary in box on page 63.

Rebecca's Well, originally Rebra's, was the spring from which the Crazies Hill women drew their water. A curate of Wargrave, Grenville Phillimore, organised funding for a proper brick bowl in 1870 and renamed the well after Isaac's wife.

Remenham is RAMEHA in the Berkshire section of the Domesday Book. The parish occupies most of the horse-shoe bend in the river. The church is largely Victorian but parts of the walls go back to the 12th century. A moat on the opposite side of the lane, in Remenham Farm, was probably the site of an early manor house. From Saxon, *ham* denotes a homestead and *hamm*, watery land. Either could apply. *Rima* was a border. The river is the county border and could have been the international boundary of Wessex & Mercia.

Romney Lock was first built in 1797 to ease navigation at Windsor Bridge.

Royal Lodge started as the Lower Lodge, home of Deputy Rangers but was rebuilt as a temporary home for George IV while he waited for Cumberland Lodge to be made ready; he stayed on. In 1931 it was rebuilt again for the Duke of York (later George VI) who was the Ranger. He encouraged Eric Savill to develop the Savill Garden (1932) and built The Village for estate workers. It became the retirement home of the Dowager Queen Elizabeth (the late Queen Mother) and is now the official residence of HRH the Duke of York.

Ruscombe, now an appendage of Twyford, is first documented in the founding charter of Salisbury Cathedral which, in 1067, received Sonning Church with 10 hides of land at *Rosecamp*. It became a manor for one of the prebends. There is written evidence for a chapel at Ruscombe in 1185 which may have become the church. A late Norman scalloped piscina uncovered in 1984 and the lancet windows of the flint chancel could be of that date. The brick nave was built in 1638 and the fine brick tower around the same time.

St Patrick's Stream is one of several outlets of the River Loddon to the Thames but the water flows into it and back out through the others. Shiplake Lock is between the outlets and the weir has raised the upstream water level.

Shiplake is not a Domesday Book name but probably corresponds to the large manor of LACHEBROC (12 hides), now represented by Lashbrook Farm which is adjacent to the main residential part, Lower Shiplake. The Twyford-Henley railway came across the river in 1854 with a station which caused expansion. The estate houses clustered around Shiplake Court, near the church, became Upper Shiplake. There had been a great house here since at least 1265 and it was the home of the Englefields in Tudor times. The estate fell into disarray and the big house was pulled down in 1808. Shiplake Court was rebuilt in 1894 and later became the site of Shiplake College. The church is where Tennyson was married in 1850 to Emily Sellwood, a cousin of the vicar's wife. He had some difficulty wooing her for poetry was not profitable and he was not yet Lord or Laureate. The south aisle is the nave of 1140. Richard of Cornwall (brother of Henry III) owned the manor and added the present nave in the next century. The stone pillar with carved heads just inside the door is 14th century.

Shiplake College is a young independent school which opened in 1959. The 40-roomed house had been previously owned by the BBC which intended it for overseas broadcasting but changed its corporate mind.

Shottesbrooke was probably cut off from the Waltham Manor in 1007 and has its own entry in the Domesday Book as SOTESBROC. A clearing in Windsor Forest, it was held by a family of goldsmiths before and after the Conquest; the forest would have supplied charcoal. The medieval village has been lost and may well have been a scattered community in the woods. Lords of the Manor in the 18th & 19th centuries were the Vansittarts; from 1886, the Smiths. The house, Shottesbrooke Park is the 16th century manor house built by the Earl of Oxford. The diapering is original. The original windows had stone surrounds but were altered around 1710 to accommodate new-fangled sash windows. The hoods over the windows and the castellation are Victorian Gothic.

Shottesbrooke Church, St John the Baptist, has a wonderful sense of space and is largely unaltered English Decorated. It probably stands on the site of the Saxon church listed in the Domesday Book and a Norman Church but the present church was built in 1337 as part of a monastic college. The spire and roof had to be rebuilt after a lightning strike in 1757. Points of interest: the elegant silhouette seen from afar; the almost equal length of nave, chancel and transepts; founder's tomb of 1363 in the north transept; brasses for an unidentified priest and frankelein (a low order of freeman) c1370, Margaret Pennebrygg (daughter of founder Sir William Trussell) 1401, Richard Gyll in armour with misericord & sword (Sergeant of the Bakehouse to Henry VII & VIII) 1511, Thomas Noke (with yeoman's badge on his left shoulder) and his three wives, 1567. The college was dissolved by 1546. It was on the site of the farm buildings on the south side which are now headquarters of *Landmark*, the historic buildings trust.   *Monumental Brasses of of Berkshire* H T Morley 1924 262pp

The **Silk Mill** on the Loddon at Twyford is now apartments, replacing the industrial buildings destroyed by fire in 1976. It appears to have been a flour mill most of the time but additionally made silk for about 10 years until 1830. Its earliest certain date is 1363. It was milling animal food when it closed.

Smith's Lawn is now a venue for polo matches and the base of the Guards Club. Smith is said to have been the riding master of the young Duke of Cumberland. During the Great War it was a Canadian Forestry Corps camp for making military huts. Edward VIII had an airstrip here. In the Second World War II it became an airfield for heavy aircraft.

Sonning like many other places derives its *-ing* from Saxon *-ingas* denoting the name of a people, clan, gang or family, who occupied the area. Sunninghill takes its name from the same people. The earliest known Saxon charter (for a grant of land to Chertsey Abbey, around 673) uses the land of the *Sunninges* as the boundary. A charter of 964 was signed by Osulf, bishop Sunnungensis. The Domesday Book SONINGES was large: land for 46 ploughs, woodland rated at 300 pigs, 5 fisheries. The bishop's palace was on the bluff above the river now called Holme Park, the site of Reading Blue Coat School. Elizabeth I exchanged land with the Bishop of Salisbury to obtain the manor. Charles I sold it after which it was owned by a succession of wealthy merchants or industrialists. *The Bull* is a 16th century building on church land; probably the site of the Bishop's guest house. Dick Turpin had an aunt who lived at *The Dog*. Story has it he visited her in order to leave his horse and escape over the river to Oxfordshire.   *The Book of Sonning* Angela Perkins 1977 Barracuda 160pp

Sonning Church is very large and once held a bishop's throne. Remnants of 12th century work are hidden by later additions but most of the fabric is pre-1400. In the wall of the tower are carved stones from the earlier building. The Saxon dioceses of Winchester and Sherborne were reorganised in 909 to form additional dioceses: Wells, Crediton and Ramsbury. Florence of Worcester (a monk) refers to Ramsbury bishops as Bishops of Ramsbury and Sonning and gives the list which is displayed in the church starting in 909 with Athelstan. There was a palace of the bishops before and after the Norman Conquest.

Sonning Bridge is of uncertain age but assumed to be 18th century. There is a tradition of a wooden bridge here in 1125 but no hard evidence. Documents refer to repairing a timber bridge in 1594.

Sonning Lock was the highest of the first eight pound locks built for the Thames Commissioners. It opened in 1773 when the charge was 1d per ton. At that time horsing for 100 ton barge was 3 shillings per mile. The mills and fisheries in the Domesday Book imply there was some kind of weir in 1086.

The **Sounding Arch** is the broadest brick span in the world, 128' with a rise of only 24½', one of Brunel's innovations. The Thames Commissioners insisted the barge channel and tow path be in the same arch. Turner's painting, *Wind, Steam and Speed* (1844) has a fast train crossing it above a sluggish boat.

Sir Stanley **Spencer**, 1891-1959, lived and painted in Cookham for most of his life. His independent work was mainly religious and/or Cookham scenes, increasingly *faux-naïf* , but he also executed many commissions and was an official war artist in both world wars. He was born at a house in High Street and his grave is in the churchyard. The art gallery in High Street is devoted to his work.   *Stanley Spencer* Duncan Robinson 1990 Phaidon 128pp

Stanlake Park is known today for its vineyard. The first vines were planted in 1979. The several wines are made on the estate and more varieties of grapes are grown than any other English vineyard. The Stanlakes estate, from which the Park was detached in 1850, probably came about in 1470 by the marriage of a Stanlake to the heiress of Hinton Pipard. This was a manor cleaved from the Earl of Salisbury's large manor of Hinton first heard of in 1166.

Stubbings appears to have been detached as an estate from Bisham. It became a parish in the 1850s when the church, St James the Less, was built. Lord Dorchester, 1724-1808, lived at Stubbings House; he was CinC British Forces in America after the War of Independence then Governor of Quebec. Queen Wilhelmina of the Netherlands lived here in exile during World War II.

Tæppa Hloew, in the old churchyard at Taplow Court, is a 7th century burial mound which in 1883 yielded the richest Saxon funerary treasure yet found (surpassed by the Sutton Hoo excavation in 1939). The Saxons used the word *barrow* for earlier burial mounds but *hloew* for their own. Presumably Tæppa was a king or chief. There is no historical record of a Tæppa living here but it was a Saxon personal name and *Taplow* provides the circumstantial evidence.

Taplow is on a chalk spur of the Chilterns. Much of the modern Taplow is an industrial and residential extension of Burnham and Slough but there is still a village centre on the top of the ridge. Domesday Book THAPESLAV was in BVRNHÃ Hundred of Bochinghamscire. Its 14 ploughs indicate extensive farm land but must also have been well forested for its woodland was assessed at 700 pigs. The land would have stretched down to the Thames and its fishery was taxed @ 1000 eels. A later mill made paper and still operates using re-cycled paper. The church, St Nicholas, is a handsome Gothic-style building of 1912 with landmark spire. The medieval church was beside Taplow Court.

Taplow Court has open days. It is a Buddhist cultural and conference centre. The splendid building, restyled Jacobean in the 19th century, dates mainly from 1700 when George Hamilton, 1st Duke of Orkney, acquired it. He appears to have become wealthy enough to buy both it and Cliveden by taking Elizabeth Villiers, mistress of William III, off the king's hands and marrying her. Bapsey Pond in the garden is said to be where the Birinus baptised converts.

Temple Footbridge was opened 24.5.1989 where the towing path transfers to the other side of the river and where there was a horse ferry until 1953.

Temple Mill Island was at the edge of the Knights Templar estate of Bisham. Daniel Defoe, in 1708, described three mills on the island. They were copper and brass mills making kitchen utensils and must have been smelting, for the freight of ore from London was listed as 18 shillings per ton in 1793. The mills were making copper for ships' bottoms in 1800 but had become paper mills by 1900. Temple Lock had a winch and fishery in 1544 and became one of the original eight pound locks in 1773. The collector was then paid 5s 6d weekly.

The **Thames Path** opened in 1996, a long distance route of 180 miles from the source in Gloucestershire through London to the Thames Barrier.

Twyford was described as a *praty townlet* by Leland, Henry VIII's Antiquary, in his tour of England around 1540. It was not big enough to become a parish until 1876. The church, St Mary, was built in 1847. The town derived trade from the Bath and Bristol highway and industry from the mills on the Loddon.

Victoria Bridge was new in 1851.

Waltham Place has gardens, a farm shop and tea room open in summer. Built about 1634 it is the manor house of the White Waltham estate carved from the larger Domesday Book holding. William Neile FRS, 1637-70, lived and died here (the first mathematician to rectify the cubical parabola, 1659). Since 1910 the estate has been owned by the Oppenheimer family.

Warren Row, originally a hamlet of Hurley, has a tunnel into the chalk for the former whiting factory. It was used as an underground factory for aircraft parts in World War II then became an emergency Regional Seat of Government.

White Waltham corresponds to two of the three manors of WALTHA listed in the Domesday Book, a large one of 10 hides belonged to Chertsey Abbey for the household supplies of the monks and a small one of 3 hides, to the Bishop of Durham. These were probably sub-divisions of the grant of 30 hides at Wealdham by King Edmund in 940 to his thegn Ælfsige. Smaller estates were carved from White Waltham in the 13th century and the rest was sold off after the Dissolution. The church, St Mary the Virgin, may be on the site of the Domesday Book church. It has undergone much rebuilding. Points of interest: three original lancet windows in the 13th century chancel, a 12th century arch under the tower.   *The Churches of Wealdham* Luke Over White Waltham PCC 16pp

White Waltham Airfield was the De Haviland Flying School before World War II and became the ATA (Air Transport Auxillary) HQ during the war, the base for aircraft ferry pilots. As West London Aero Club it now offers training in basic flying and ærial acrobatics.

Windsor in the Domesday Book is Old Windsor. The present Windsor should probably be called Clewer because it developed on the land of the Domesday Book manor of Clewer. It took its name from the castle which took its name from the royal palace at old Windsor. The town grew up around the castle.

Windsor Bridge is now pedestrianised. In its early days it was a private enterprise. Osbert de Bray took £4 6s 6d in tolls in 1172 for vessels passing through his bridge. In 1735 downward barges had to pay a 6d toll to defray shipping damage. In 1769 a law forbade the navigators to jeopardise the users of Thames Street and a winch was installed to draw barges up to the bridge. The present bridge was built around 1823. In 1367 the London-Windsor freight charge for coal (from Newcastle) was 1 shilling per chaldron (36 bushels). An Eton boy's letter of 1470 refers to a parcel arriving by barge. Around 1800, 40 tons of freight were unloaded at Windsor daily; the passenger fare was 2s from London. The king's water engine was built on the bank in 1681 to drive water up to the castle. The queen's turbines currently supply electricity to the castle.

Windsor Castle can be seen as a distant landmark from many walks in this book. It was founded by William the Conqueror as a timber and earth fort on a chalk bluff above the Thames. The earliest record of it as a residence is in the 1110s when, according to the Chronicles of Abingdon, Henry I made a grant to the monks *apud Castillum Uiildesores*. It has been a royal home ever since, being rebuilt in stone around 1250. Additions have been made to it in every century.   *Windsor - the most romantic castle* Mark Giruard 1993 Hodder & Stoughton 160pp

WGP notes for newcomers to Windsor Great Park:
Windsor Great Park has no public rights-of-way but the Crown Estate permits walkers to wander. Paths in the maps are tarmac, gravel or grass. It is possible to cut across grass and woods between paths but ditches may intervene. There are private areas for residences and farming. Estate policy is to keep walkers and horses apart so horse tracks should be left to riders who pay for the privilege. In most parts horse tracks can be followed over the grass nearby.

The free parking areas near the gates fill up during public holidays.

The deer fence has gates only where paths and roads cross it. Red deer stags should be treated with caution during the rut - autumn. Isolated deer calves are not lost; touching them causes them to be abandoned. Dogs must be on leads.

Windsor Great Park was probably detached from Windsor Forest about 1246 when Henry III built the Great Manor as a family home adjacent to the Devil's Highway and Windlel Stream (now under Virginia Water). The Forest extended west to the Blackwater and Loddon rivers and south to the Hog's Back. The original Great Park reached only a little way north of the Savill Garden and was not extended to the castle until the Park was restored to Charles II. On Snow Hill, Henry VIII awaited a gunshot at the Castle to signal the beheading of Anne Boleyn. The Copper Horse bears George III attired as Marcus Aurelius. It was ordered by George IV, designed by Richard Westmacott, made from 25 brass guns and erected in 1831. The statue is 25½ feet tall and the granite pedestal 27 feet. The Long Walk is 2½ miles long and was begun in 1680 by Charles II. It was originally 240 feet wide. Queen Anne's Ride was planted with elms around 1708 to provide a route to Ascot for the queen in her hunting chaise.
Royal Landscape - gardens & parks of Windsor J Roberts 1997 Yale UP 596pp

Winkfield was WINECANFELDA in a 942 charter of Edmund, king of Wessex, who granted it (with Swinley) to a holy woman, Sæthryth. In 1015 it was given to Abingdon Abbey. It is WENESFELLE in the Domesday Book. The settlement is non-nuclear, probably because of its forest origin where homesteads may have been scattered in the woods. The hamlets within the parish are Winkfield Row, Winkfield Street, Cranbourne and Chevey Down. Ascot expanded on the original manor land. Various estates cut out of the forest, associated with the royal neighbourhood, have added themselves to the parish which is large and prosperous: Foliejon, Winkfield Place, Ascot Place and New Lodge. The church, St Mary's, has puddingstone walls of about 1300, though there was an earlier church. The flint rubble chancel is entirely Victorian. Points of interest: the spaciousness of the (rare) double nave and lightweight roof of the Tudor rebuilding; the front oak pillar carved with a Tudor rose, 1592 and ER; the early brick tower with *1629* on a brick; the brass behind the pulpit; memorials to august estate owners.   *The History of Winkfield* J Harris & G M Stanton 1971 124pp

Wooburn in the Domesday Book was the manor WABURNE of the Bishop of Lincoln rated for 8½ hides and 8 mills. The 18th & 19th century successors of these mills on the River Wye turned the parish into a major paper producer and it continues its industrial tradition. The manor house was the bishop's palace with the Wye artificially bent into a moat; the bishops' park became the town park. Settlement was at the church and the Green, hence Wooburn Town and Wooburn Green The church, St Paul, was founded in the 12th century but is much rebuilt. Points of interest: the elaborate rood screen and several brasses.
Theirs were but human hearts Brian Brenchley Wheals 1983 HS Publishing 176pp

The **Woodley Aircraft Museum** of Berkshire Aviation Trust opens part-time. It is mainly about the Miles Aircraft Company which built aircraft at Woodley Airfield and other plane makers. This is where Douglas Bader lost his legs.